for 9 - 11s

Book 6

CF4•K

> **We believe** that the Bible is God's word to mankind, and that it contains everything we need to know in order to be reconciled with God and live in a way that is pleasing to him. Therefore, we believe it is vital to teach children accurately from the Bible, being careful to teach each passage's true meaning in an appropriate way for children, rather than selecting a 'children's message' from a Biblical passage.

© TnT Ministries
29 Buxton Gardens, Acton, London, W3 9LE
Tel: +44 (0)20 8992 0450; Fax: +44 (0)20 8896 1847; e-mail: sales@tntministries.org.uk;
www.tntministries.org.uk

Published in 2001, reprinted 2008 by Christian Focus Publications,
Geanies House, Fearn, Tain, Ross-shire, IV20 1TW, U.K.

Tel: +44 (0)1862 871 011 Fax: +44 (0)1862 871 699
e-mail: info@christianfocus.com
www.christianfocus.com

Cover design by Douglas McConnach
This book and others in the series can be purchased from your local Christian bookshop. Alternatively you can write to TnT Ministries direct or place your order with the publisher.

ISBN 978-1-85792-556-2

Free licence is given to copy visual aids and activity pages for use as class material only. We ask that each person teaching the material purchases their own copy. Unauthorised copying and distribution is prohibited.

Scripture quotations are taken from the HOLY BIBLE, NEW INTERNATIONAL VERSION.Copyright © 1973, 1978, 1984 by International Bible Society. Used by permission of Hodder & Stoughton Publishers, A member of the Hodder Headline Group.All rights reserved. "NIV" is a registered trademark of International Bible Society.

TnT Ministries (which stands for Teaching and Training Ministries) was launched in February 1993 by Christians from a broad variety of denominational backgrounds who were concerned that teaching the Bible to children be taken seriously. The leaders were in charge of the Sunday School of 50 teachers at St Helen's Bishopgate, an evangelical church in the city of London, for 13 years, during which time a range of Biblical teaching materials was developed. TnT Ministries also runs training days for Sunday School teachers.
www.tntministries.org.uk

Christian Focus Publications publishes books for adults and children under its four main imprints: Christian Focus, Christian Heritage, CF4K and Mentor. Our books reflect that God's word is reliable and Jesus is the way to know him, and live for ever with him. Our children's publication list includes a Sunday school curriculum that covers pre-school to early teens; puzzle and activity books. We also publish personal and family devotional titles, biographies and inspirational stories that children will love. If you are looking for quality Bible teaching for children then we have an excellent range of Bible story and age specific theological books. From pre-school to teenage fiction, we have it covered!
www.christianfocus.com

CONTENTS
On the Way for 9-11s / Book 6

WEEK	SUBJECT	PAGE

THE HOLY SPIRIT - overview 6
1. *Truly God* 8
2. *Teacher* 13
3. *Counsellor* 16
4. *Signs of the New Birth* 19
5. *Harmonious Relationships* 23
6. *Control of the Sinful Nature* 27

APOLOGETICS
7. *The Existence of God* 30

HOW GOD SHOULD BE WORSHIPPED - overview 35
8. *The Tabernacle* 37
9. *Sacrifice* 47
10. *Feasts* 53
11. *The New Covenant* 60
12. *Daily Life* 64

JOB AND THE PROBLEM OF SUFFERING - overview 70
13. *Job* 71
14. *The Problem of Suffering* 76

Preparation of Bible material:
Thalia Blundell
Annie Gemmill

Editing:
David Jackman

Other Contributers:
Naomi Beak
Roz Beak
Thalia Blundell
Leona Derkson
Annie Gemmill

On the Way for 9-11s works on a two year syllabus, consisting of 6 books. It follows on from **On The Way for 3-9s** and includes material that is not covered in that syllabus. It is designed to introduce children of this age group to simple Bible study.

The lessons are grouped in series, each of which is introduced by a series overview stating the aims of the series, the lesson aim for each week and an appropriate memory verse.

Every lesson, in addition to an aim, has study notes to enable the teacher to understand the Bible passage, suggested visual aids where appropriate and an activity for the children to do and take home. Because of the emphasis on teaching basic Bible study skills, many of the activities take the form of work-sheets. These provide opportunities for applying the lessons learnt. Many of the lessons also include a craft activity.

How to Prepare a Lesson

To prepare a Sunday School lesson properly takes at least one evening (2-3 hours). It is helpful to read the Bible passage several days before teaching it to allow time to mull over what it is saying.

When preparing a lesson the following steps should be taken -

1. PRAY!

In a busy world this is very easy to forget. We are unable to understand God's word without his help and we need to remind ourselves of that fact before we start.

2. READ THE BIBLE PASSAGE

This should be done *before* reading the lesson manual. Our resource is the Bible, not what someone says about it. The Bible study notes in the lesson manual are a commentary on the passage to help you understand it.

3. LOOK AT THE LESSON AIM

This should reflect the main teaching of the passage. Plan how that can be packaged appropriately for the age group you teach.

4. TEACHING THE BIBLE PASSAGE

This should take place in the context of simple Bible study. Do ensure that the children use the same version of the Bible. Prior to the lesson decide how the passage will be read, (e.g. one verse at a time), and who should do the reading. Is the passage short enough to read the whole of it or should some parts be paraphrased by the teacher? Work through the passage, deciding which points should be raised. Design simple questions to bring out the main teaching of the passage. The first questions should elicit the facts and should be designed so that they cannot be answered by a simple 'no' or 'yes'. If a child reads out a Bible verse as the answer, praise him/her and then ask him/her to put it in his/her own words. Once the facts have been established go on to application questions, encouraging the children to think through how the teaching can be applied to their lives. Do remember that this age group can know all the answers - it is the application of their Bible knowledge to behaviour that is so difficult!

5. VISUAL AIDS

Pictures are very rarely required for this age group. A Bible Time Line is useful so that the children can see where the Bible passage they are studying comes in the big picture of God's revelation to his people. (A Bible Time Line can be found on pages 78-79). A map is helpful to demonstrate distances, etc. Pictures and models are only required for topics such as the Tabernacle, where it is difficult to visualise what is happening from reading the Bible passage. A flip chart or similar is handy to summarise the lesson.

6. CRAFT ACTIVITIES AND WORK-SHEETS

These are designed to help the children understand and remember what they have learned. The work-sheets help the children to study the Bible passage and should be used as a teaching aid. It is not essential for the children to fill in all the gaps every week. The craft activity can be used either to lead into the lesson or as a follow-up activity. Very little prior preparation is required by the teacher.

Benefits of On The Way

- Encourages the leaders to study the Bible for themselves.

- Teaches the children simple Bible-study skills.

- Everything you need is in the one book, so there is no need to buy children's activity books.

- Undated materials allow you to use the lessons to fit your situation without wasting materials.

- Once you have the entire syllabus, there is no need to repurchase.

Teaching Simple Bible Study Skills

On The Way for 9-11s is designed to teach children of this age group how to read and understand a passage of Scripture. The children are presented with questions that require them to go to the Bible passage or to the provided cross-references for the answers (see How to Prepare a Lesson).

Before learning how to study the Bible children need to know what it is and how to find their way around it.

The Bible
Christians believe that the Bible is God's word and contains all we need to know in order to live in relationship with God and with each other. It is the way God has chosen to reveal himself to mankind; it not only records historical facts but also interprets those facts. It is not a scientific text book.

What does the Bible consist of?
The Bible is God's story. It is divided into 2 sections - the Old and New Testaments. 'Testament' means 'covenant' or 'promise'.

The Old Testament contains 39 books covering the period from creation to about 400 years before the birth of Jesus. It records God's mighty acts of creation, judgment and mercy as well as their interpretation through the words of the prophets.

The New Testament is made up of 27 books containing details of the life, death and resurrection of Jesus, the spread of the gospel in the early Church, Christian doctrine and the final judgment.

Who wrote the Bible?
The books of the Bible were written by many different people, some known and others not. Christians believe that all these authors were inspired by God (2 Peter 1:20-21, 2 Timothy 3:16). As a result we can trust what it says.

How can we find our way around it?
Each book in the Bible is divided into chapters, each one of which contains a number of verses. When the Books were written originally the chapter and verse divisions were absent. These have been added to enable the readers to find their way around. When written down they are recorded in the following way, Genesis 5:1-10. This tells us to look up the book of Genesis, chapter 5, verses 1 to 10.

At the front of the Bible is a contents page, listing the books in the order in which they come in the Bible. It is perfectly acceptable to look up the index to see which page to turn to.

Aids to teach the Bible passage
- Many of the lessons have activity pages that help to bring out the main teaching of the Bible passage.
- Packs of maps and charts can be purchased from Christian book shops.
- A Bible Time Line is useful to reinforce the chronology of the Bible (see pages 78-79).

Questions to aid in understanding
Periodically use the following questions to help the children understand the passage:
- Who wrote it?
- To whom was it written?
- When was it written?
- What situation is being described? (if applicable)

The Bible Library

To make a chart of the Bible Library enlarge the template below and photocopy as required. Draw 2 sets of shelves on a large piece of paper (see diagram). Label the shelves. Cut off the unwanted books from each set and write the names of the books on the spines. Glue the books onto the appropriate shelves in the order in which they appear in the Bible.

The Bible Library

Old Testament	New Testament
Law (5 books)	Gospels & Acts (5)
History (12 books)	Paul's Epistles (13)
Poetry & Wisdom (5)	Other Epistles (8)
Prophets (17 books)	Prophecy (1 book)

The Holy Spirit

Week 1   **TRULY GOD**   *John 14:15-31, Matthew 28:18-20, Romans 8:9-10, 2 Corinthians 1:21-22*
To understand that the Holy Spirit is God and that he is present in the life of every Christian.

Week 2   **TEACHER**   *John 14:15-31; 15:18-27*
To understand that the Holy Spirit bears witness to Jesus.

Week 3   **COUNSELLOR**   *John 15:18 - 16:16*
To understand the Holy Spirit's role in encouraging and strengthening the Christian.

Week 4   **SIGNS OF THE NEW BIRTH**   *Galatians 5:16-26, John 14:23-27; 15:9-17*
To understand what it means to 'live by the Spirit'.

Week 5   **HARMONIOUS RELATIONSHIPS**   *Galatians 5:16-26; 6:7-10, James 5:7-11, Colossians 3:12-14*
To understand what it means to 'live by the Spirit'.

Week 6   **CONTROL OF THE SINFUL NATURE**   *Galatians 5:16-26, Joshua 24:14, 3 John 2-8, Colossians 3:12-14, Titus 2:11-14, 1 Peter 3:15-16*
To understand what is means to 'live by the Spirit'.

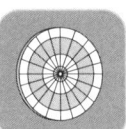

To understand the basic doctrines regarding the person and work of the Holy Spirit.

This series looks at the work of the Holy Spirit in the lives of all believers. The first 3 lessons study the Upper Room discourse in John 14-16, where Jesus sets out for his disciples the future work of the Holy Spirit in teaching and reminding them of everything Jesus had said to them (John 14:26). The last three lessons look at the work of the Holy Spirit in sanctifying the Christian, as found in Galatians 5:16-25.

In order to teach this series effectively it is important to understand what the Bible has to say about the person and work of the Holy Spirit.

1. The Holy Spirit is the third person of the Godhead (Matthew 28:18-20). In the Upper Room Jesus tells his disciples that the Father will send them the Holy Spirit (John 14:16-17) and equates this with Jesus coming to them (John 14:18).

2. The Holy Spirit is present in the life of every Christian (Acts 2:38-39, Romans 8:9, Titus 3:4-7).

3. The presence of the Holy Spirit is an assurance of salvation (1 John 4:13, 2 Corinthians 1:21-22).

4. The Holy Spirit makes the believer more Christ-like (sanctification) - 2 Corinthians 3:17-18, 1 Thessalonians 4:3-8, Galatians 5:16-25. This is a gradual work and goes on throughout life.

5. The Holy Spirit strengthens and encourages the believer (John 15:26 - 16:4). The word Counsellor means Comforter (strengthener) and Advocate (one who presents your case in court and fights alongside you).

6. The Holy Spirit reveals God to the believer so that he or she might know God better (Ephesians 1:17, John 16:12-15). He does this by inspiration and illumination of the Scriptures (Hebrews 3:7, 1 Peter 1:10-11, 2 Peter 1:21).

NB. It is important to remember that the Holy Spirit is part of the Godhead and, although it simplifies things to talk about each member having a specific role, (i.e. the Father - creation, the Son - redemption, and the Spirit - sanctification), it is not possible to separate completely the work of one member from the work of the other two. Thus the Bible speaks of God the Father creating the world (Genesis 1:1), the Son being involved in creation (John 1:3) and the Holy Spirit also being involved (Genesis 1:2; 1:26 - use of the plural). In the same way, the work of sanctification is applied to the Holy Spirit in 2 Corinthians 3:17-18, and to Jesus in Ephesians 5:26-27.

Any work of the Spirit that does not bring glory to Jesus Christ must be suspect.

The fruit of the Spirit is love, joy, peace, patience, kindness, goodness, faithfulness, gentleness and self-control.

Galatians 5:22-23

WEEK 1
Truly God

Preparation:
Read John 14:15-31, Matthew 28:18-20, Romans 8:9-10, 2 Corinthians 1:21-22 using the Bible Study notes to help you.

Lesson Aim:
To understand that the Holy Spirit is God and that he is present in the life of every Christian.

This study (and those for the next 2 weeks) looks at part of the discourse Jesus addressed to his disciples in the upper room prior to his arrest and crucifixion. It follows after Jesus' prediction of his betrayal and Peter's denial that he would forsake Jesus, and comes at a time when the disciples are feeling confused and despondent.

John

14:16   Counsellor means comforter and advocate (see series overview). Jesus is our advocate with the Father (1 John 2:1). The Holy Spirit is Jesus' advocate with us.

14:17   Spirit of truth - see John 15:26; 16:13.

14:18   Jesus will come by means of the Holy Spirit.

14:19   Refers to the resurrection. See 1 Corinthians 15:12-19.

14:21   Obeying Jesus' commands (words) is inextricably linked with love for Christ. Our love is demonstrated by obedience.

14:23   Note the link with verse 17. The Father and Son will make their home with the believer (v.23), as will the Holy Spirit (v.17).

14:24   Jesus equates his words with the Father's words - he only speaks what the Father speaks.

14:26   This was written primarily to the disciples, who literally heard Jesus' words. The Holy Spirit would remind them of all that Jesus had said - a great assurance for us that the Scriptures are trustworthy! (See also point 6 in the series aims).

14:30   The Prince of this world is Satan (cf. John 12:30-33).

Matthew

28:19   The Holy Spirit is part of the Godhead, in whose name all disciples are commanded to be baptised.

Romans

8:9-10   The Holy Spirit lives in every believer. We must not divide Jesus and the Holy Spirit. He is called the Spirit (v.9), the Spirit of God (v.9), the Spirit of Christ (v.9), Christ (v.10).

2 Corinthians

1:21-22   God has placed his Holy Spirit in each Christian as a guarantee that we belong to him.

Use a pen and paper puzzle e.g. hangman, to get the words 'Holy Spirit'. Ask the children what they know about the Holy Spirit and list their answers on a board or flip chart. If your group is likely to know very little you could ask them simple questions about the Holy Spirit that require true or false as the answer, e.g. the Holy Spirit is God, the Holy Spirit was promised to us by Abraham, etc. In today's Bible passage we will see what Jesus had to say about the Holy Spirit.

Teach the passage using the activity pages to help you. Do not teach the memory verse this week, because there is a memory verse puzzle as part of next week's session. At the end of the study summarize what the children have learned about the Holy Spirit and compare that with what they knew at the beginning.

Photocopy page 10 on coloured card and pages 11 and 12 on paper for each child. Each child also requires 1 sheet of A4 coloured card for the back cover and an A4 slide binder. Prior to the lesson cut out a flame shape for each child from red paper for them to glue onto the front cover (see diagram).

Divide the children into twos or threes and ask them to use the letters HOLY SPIRIT to devise an acrostic dealing with the person and work of the Holy Spirit. E.g. H - holy, O - obedience, etc. If they cannot think of a word starting with the letter, they can use a word that contains that letter, e.g. Y - joy. Ask the groups to feed back to each other at the end.

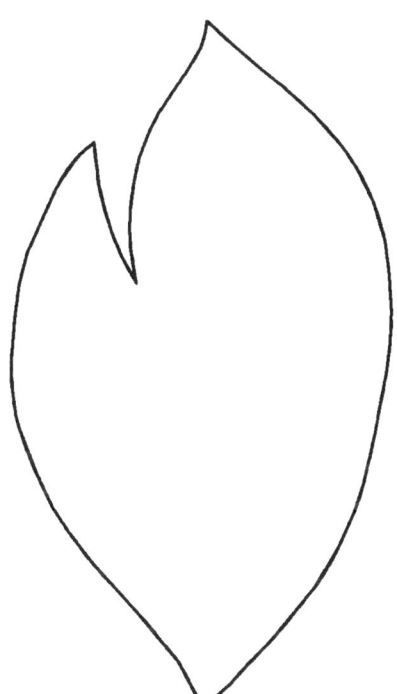

The Holy Spirit

Truly God

John 14:15-31

This passage is part of the talk Jesus gave to his disciples in the upper room on the night he was arrested. It follows the washing of the disciples' feet and the Last Supper. Jesus had told his disciples that he would be leaving them (John 13:33-38) and they were feeling sad (14:1). In this passage Jesus tells them about the Holy Spirit, who will come to be with the disciples in Jesus' place.

What name does Jesus give to the Holy Spirit?

* C.............................. (v.16)

* S.................. of T...................... (v.17)

What does Counsellor mean?

Starting at the arrow, write down every third letter in the spaces below to discover 3 words to help you to understand the meaning.

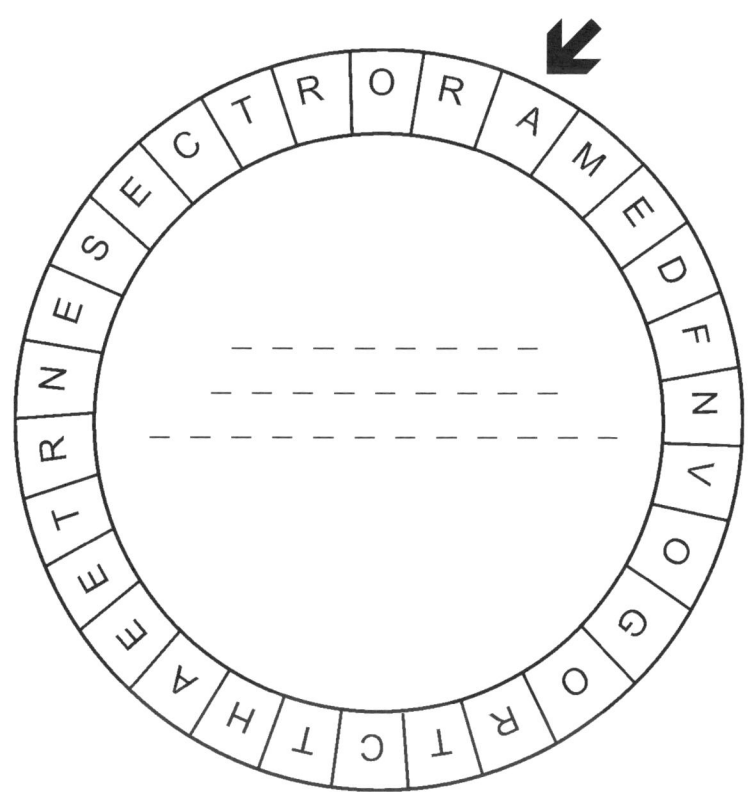

In verses 16-17, who does Jesus say will come to live in the disciples forever?

....

But -

in verses 18-20, Jesus says that **HE** will come to live in his disciples.

Is Jesus saying that the disciples will have **2** people living in them?

Read Matthew 28:18-20. Here Jesus talks about the Holy Spirit as being part of the G _ _ _ _ _ _ , in whose name all disciples are commanded to be baptised.

Does this mean that the Holy Spirit is God?   ☐ yes   ☐ no

Now look at John 14:23 to see who else will make his home with the believer

the F _ _ _ _ _ .

In John 14:16-17, Jesus promised to send the Holy Spirit to his disciples. Was this promise only for the twelve?

Read Romans 8:9-10 and 2 Corinthians 1:21-22. Does the Holy Spirit live in **every** believer or only in some?

Thank God for giving his Holy Spirit to **every** believer as a guarantee of our salvation.

WEEK 2
Teacher

Preparation:
Read John 14:15-31; 15:18-27, using the Bible Study notes to help you.

Lesson Aim:
To understand that the Holy Spirit bears witness to Jesus.

14:15-31   See notes for week 1.

15:18-20   By following Jesus, the believer has set himself in opposition to the world. Persecution as a Christian is a mark of our belonging to Jesus.

15:26   The Holy Spirit comes from both the Father and the Son - 'I will send,' 'goes out from the Father'.

15:27   The witnesses will also point people to Jesus. Note that this verse was written to the disciples - they were the ones who were with Jesus from the beginning. We are only witnesses in a secondary way, i.e. to testify to what the disciples witnessed and wrote down. The witness is to Jesus, not to the Holy Spirit.

recommended). In today's Bible passage we will see if we can trust the Holy Spirit to teach us the truth about Jesus.

Teach the Bible passage, using the activity pages to help you. Teach the memory verse after the activity pages have been completed. At the end of the lesson compare what they have learned about the Holy Spirit with what they decided about trusting their teacher to teach accurately.

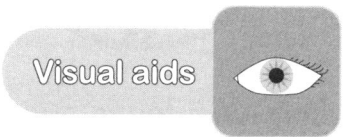

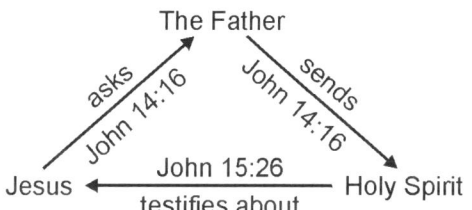

Photocopy pages 14 and 15 for each child and add to the back of the activity book.

Ask the children to describe their ideal teacher. List the attributes on a board or flip chart. Ask, 'What do you think are the most important things about a good teacher?' Elicit such things as trustworthy, teaches the truth, is understandable, etc. Talk about the importance of being able to trust their teacher to teach accurately. Discuss how they know that they can trust their teacher to do this, bringing out their knowledge of the teacher, the teacher's previous record and the teacher's credentials (comes

Teacher

John 14:15-31; 15:18-27

Jesus told his disciples that the Holy Spirit would do the following -

* ✻ t..................... them all things (14:26)

* ✻ r..................... them of everything that Jesus had told them (14:26)

* ✻ t..................... about J......................... (15:26)

If this is what the Holy Spirit is to do, why is it important that he is called the Spirit of Truth? (14:17)

Who was Jesus speaking to in 14:26?   ☐ the disciples

☐ every Christian

How does this verse help us to believe what we read in the Bible?

Who does the Holy Spirit bear witness to? (15:26)   ☐ himself

☐ Jesus

When people say that the Holy Spirit has told them something, how does this verse help us to decide if what they say is true?

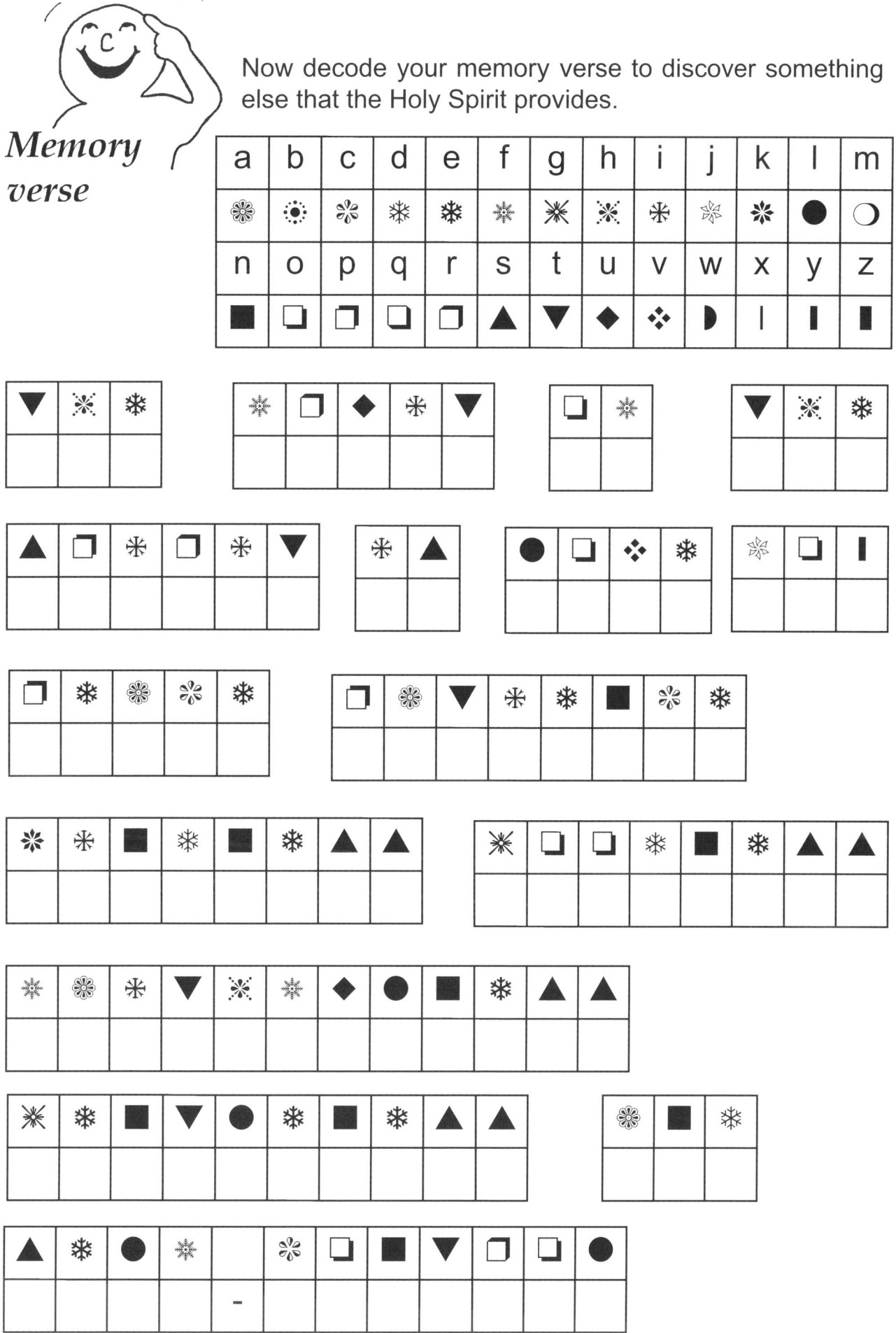

WEEK 3
Counsellor

Preparation:
Read John 15:18 - 16:16 using the Bible Study notes to help you.

Lesson Aim:
To understand the Holy Spirit's role in encouraging and strengthening the Christian.

15:18-27 See notes for week 2.

16:2 See Acts 8:1-3.

16:7 'Go' means go to the Father (John 14:5,12). The dispensation of the Holy Spirit was dependent on Jesus' glorification and victory over sin (John 7:39). This verse does not mean that Jesus and the Holy Spirit cannot be present at the same time.

16:8-11 The work of the Holy Spirit in conviction of guilt. This does not imply that the world will necessarily recognise its guilt.

16:9 Anyone who does not accept Christ's saving death on his behalf is guilty of sin and will be punished accordingly.

16:10 Jesus' righteousness is vindicated by his glorification.

16:11 Satan was defeated at the cross.

16:13 The Holy Spirit will guide the apostles into all truth - his words are the Father's words (see also John 14:24). NB, John 14:26 was a promise to the twelve and gives us a reason to trust the gospels. Memory in the ancient world was very, very good; things were continually recited. First century education was carried out by memorising. The Holy Spirit guides the 12 into all truth so that they can give us the whole Christian faith. Therefore, the Spirit cannot lead us into something that is not present in Scripture.

16:14 The Spirit's job is to bring glory to Jesus. He has no separate ministry or message.

16:16 'After a little while you will see me' refers to the resurrection.

NB. The Holy Spirit's work of sanctification will be dealt with in detail over the next 3 weeks.

Ask the children what they would do in the following situations:

1. You are on a country walk with a group of friends. About half way to the destination, one of the group wants to give up and go back.

2. One of your friends loses something precious and is very upset.

3. It is school speech day and you have been asked to stand up and give the vote of thanks to the visiting speaker. You feel very inadequate for the task.

If you have a large group of children divide them into smaller groups for the discussion, then allow them to feed back to the rest of the group. Point out that however much they encourage and comfort their friends they cannot give the inner strength needed for the task. In today's Bible passage we will discover who can do all of this.

Teach the Bible passage, using the activity pages to help you. Revise the memory verse. At the end of the Bible study remind the children that the Holy Spirit enables us to tell others about Jesus and discuss specific ways that the children can do this, e.g. plan a special event to which they can ask their friends.

Photocopy pages 17 and 18 for each child and add to the back of the activity book.

 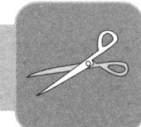

Counsellor   John 15:18 - 16:16

In John 14:26 Jesus called the Holy Spirit the Counsellor. Can you remember the 3 words that help us to understand what that means?

* A............................
* C............................
* S............................

What does Jesus promise to leave his disciples in 14:27?   p....................

What does he mean by that?

- ☐ no more arguments
- ☐ a quiet life
- ☐ no more wars
- ☐ peace with God

Read 15:18-25 and 16:1-2 to see what their lives would be like.

* h.................... by the w.................... (15:18)
* p.................... (15:20)
* put out of the s.................... (16:2)

Jesus was telling his disciples that they would not only be persecuted by the pagans but also by the religious people!

Think about the times when you are teased or bullied because you are a Christian. How does the Holy Spirit help you cope?

Read John 16:7-11. What else does the Holy Spirit do?

✱ He c.................................. the world of g...................... (v.8)

Does this mean that the world recognises its guilt? ☐ yes

☐ no

Why is the world guilty in regard to:

✱ sin? (v.9)

They do not b.............................. in Jesus.

✱ righteousness? (v.10)

They do not believe that Jesus has ascended into h.......................

✱ judgment? (v.11)

They do not believe that S.......................... has already been defeated at the cross.

Thank God for giving us his Holy Spirit to comfort and strengthen us.

18

WEEK 4
Signs of the New Birth

Preparation:
Read Galatians 5:16-26, John 14:23-27; 15:9-17 using the Bible Study notes to help you.

Lesson Aim:
To understand what it means to 'live by the Spirit'.

Galatians

5:16 The Spirit is the Holy Spirit. The sinful nature or flesh means our condition as fallen human beings.

5:17 The conflict between the Spirit and the flesh will continue until we die (see Romans 7:21-25).

5:18 The Holy Spirit is present in the lives of all believers (Romans 8:9) and, as a result, we are delivered from the penalty of the law. His ongoing work in the believer is one of sanctification (2 Corinthians 3:17-18). This verse does not mean that we do not need to keep God's law.

5:19-21 Our sinful nature is evidenced by our actions.

5:19 Deals with sexual sin.

5:20 Idolatry - offences against God. Witchcraft - any involvement with the powers of evil.

5:20-21 Hatred through to envy deal with a breakdown in society and personal relationships.

5:21 Drunkenness and orgies are to do with the abuse of alcohol and resultant loss of self-control.

Note the warning at the end of verse 21.

5:22-23 The fruit of the Spirit. The presence of the Holy Spirit in our lives is evidenced by our behaviour. Love, joy, peace will be dealt with this week (see notes at the end of this section). Patience, kindness, goodness will be looked at next week (week 5). Faithfulness, gentleness, self-control will be studied in week 6. Remember that, just as physical fruit grows slowly and steadily, so should spiritual fruit.

5:24 This verse does not imply that the Christian should not be troubled by the sinful nature, rather that he should set his face against the desires of the sinful nature, i.e. wage war against it.

5:25 'Keep in step with the Spirit'. The verb used for 'keep in step' comes from the same root as the noun used for the 'basic principles' that control us in Galatians 4:3,9. To keep in step with the Spirit is to allow his voice to be the controlling one and to seek to live by the principles laid down in Scripture.

5:26 Living by the Spirit should show itself in our dealings with each other. 'Provoke' is to challenge to a contest with the aim of demonstrating our own superiority, i.e. making others feel small and unimpressive. Provoking and envying come as a result of conceit.

Love, Joy, Peace.
These are concerned primarily with our relationships with God and are all signs of the new birth - love for God, the joy of knowing we are forgiven and peace with God.

John

15:9 We are called to remain in Jesus' love.

15:10 The key to remaining in Jesus' love is obeying his commands.

15:11 The result of this obedience is joy - both Jesus' joy in us and our joy.

15:12 We are called to love each other in the same way that Jesus loved us (sacrificially). We need to discuss with the children how this works in practice.

15:16 We are commanded to bear fruit - it is not optional.

14:23   See 15:10.

14:27   Jesus' peace is given to us, therefore we must not let our hearts be troubled or be afraid (Philippians 4:7).

Peace is harmony or concord, i.e. an absence of fighting, enmity, etc. (Galatians 5:19-21).

Start with a quiz to recap on what has been learned so far in the series. Divide the children into 2 teams. The winner is the team that collects most fruit. Pin up 2 tree outlines (one for each team) and 12 fruit shapes (see diagrams). Prepare 12 questions to bring out the main points from the previous 3 lessons. A question is put to each team in turn and, if answered correctly, one of the team members chooses a fruit and pins it onto their tree. If an incorrect answer is given the question is offered to the other team. Allow 10 minutes for the quiz.

If there are insufficient children to form 2 teams, play the children against the leader. All questions are put to the children. If they answer the question correctly they pick a fruit. If the children answer incorrectly the leader picks a fruit.

Discuss with the children what they have learned so far about the Holy Spirit - he is God, he indwells every believer, he teaches us about Jesus, he comforts and strengthens the believer, he convicts the world of sin. Tell them that the next 3 lessons will be spent looking at the Holy Spirit's work in the individual believer. Use the visual aid to demonstrate that the Holy Spirit's presence in the believer is demonstrated by what the believer does.

Teach the lesson, using the activity pages to help you. Revise the memory verse.

A glove puppet. Place it on the table. Without a hand inside it, it can do nothing. When the hand is placed inside the puppet the hand cannot be seen, but we know it is there because of the actions of the puppet. In the same way we cannot see the Holy Spirit, but the way that we live should demonstrate his presence in our lives.

Photocopy pages 21 and 22 for each child and add to the back of the activity book.

Signs of the New Birth   Galatians 5:16-26

Over the next 3 lessons we will look at the Holy Spirit's work of sanctification.

What is sanctification?

Read 2 Corinthians 3:17-18.

Sanctification is the process of making Christians more like J....................

Does it happen suddenly?   ☐ yes   ☐ no

Read Galatians 5:16-18.

Paul tells the Galatian Christians that they are in a constant battle. Should they live by the S......................... or should they follow their s....................... n.............................?

What is the sinful nature?

Am I still affected by it once I become a Christian?

Does verse 18 mean that I do not need to keep God's law?

Galatians 5:19-21 lists what can happen when the sinful nature has its own way.

Do any of these apply to you or to people you know?

What about hatred, discord, jealousy, fits of rage, etc.?

21

Can this sinful nature please God? (v.21)   ☐ yes   ☐ no

How can we stop giving in to our sinful nature? (v.16)

L...................... by the S........................

We do this when we allow the Holy Spirit to be the controlling voice in our lives.

The Holy Spirit's presence in our lives is demonstrated by our behaviour. In Galatians Paul calls this the fruit of the Spirit.
Read Galatians 5:22-23.

Love for God and for one another.

How do I show my love for God? (John 14:23)

By o........................... his commands.

John 15:12-13 tells us one of Jesus' commands. How do I put this into practice?

Joy of knowing I am forgiven.

Look at John 15:9-11. The result of obeying Jesus' commands is j........!

Does this mean that I must always look happy?

Peace with God and with each other.

Read John 14:26-27.

Which verses in Galatians 5 are the opposite of peace?

Love, joy and peace are all marks of the Christian. Do I show them in my life?

WEEK 5
Harmonious Relationships

Preparation:
Read Galatians 5:16-26; 6:7-10, James 5:7-11, Colossians 3:12-14, using the Bible Study

Lesson Aim:
To understand what it means to 'live by the Spirit'.

Galatians
5:16-26 See notes for week 4.

Patience, Kindness, Goodness.
These 3 are primarily concerned with our relationships with other people.

James
5:7 Patience means longsuffering. We are commanded to be patient. The farmer is an example of patience.

5:9 Patience in action.

5:10-11 The prophets and Job are examples of patience in the face of suffering. We are called to live in a world that is at enmity with God, but the Christian's attitude to the world must not be hostile.

Colossians
3:13 How we demonstrate the virtues described in 3:12. Kindness is graciousness, gentleness.

See 2 Samuel 9:1-13 for an example of kindness in action.

Galatians
6:9 Goodness is doing good to others. Although these qualities are given us by God, we need to work hard at their development (see also 2 Peter 1:5).

6:10 We are called to do good to all people, not just to our friends.

Start with the Quick Quiz on page 24 to get the word 'relationships'. Discuss what makes relationships go wrong, using such things as playground disagreements, sibling rivalry, etc. as examples. Wouldn't it be wonderful if we lived in a world where there were no problems with relationships? In today's Bible passage we will find out how the Holy Spirit helps us in our relationships.

Teach the Bible passage using the activity pages to help you. Revise the memory verse by making it a team game. Prior to the lesson prepare one set of memory verse words per team. Use the apple outline on page 27 and write one word of the memory verse, including the reference, on each apple. It is helpful if each team's apples are a different colour. Give each team their apples in jumbled order. The first team to put their apples in the order of the memory verse wins.

Photocopy pages 25 and 26 for each child and add to the back of the activity book.

QUICK QUIZ!

Answer the following questions and enter your answers in the grid below.

1. What is the colour of danger?
2. What can be found in a bird's nest?
3. Which animal is the King of the Beasts?
4. What is another word for 'ever'?
5. What is the second day in the school week?
6. What is the opposite of 'well'?
7. Which fruit has the same name as its colour?
8. What is the fourth book in the Old Testament?
9. What is the ninth month of the year?
10. What is another word for 'be quick'?
11. What is a cool treat on a hot day?
12. What can you write with?
13. What word is the opposite of 'weak'?

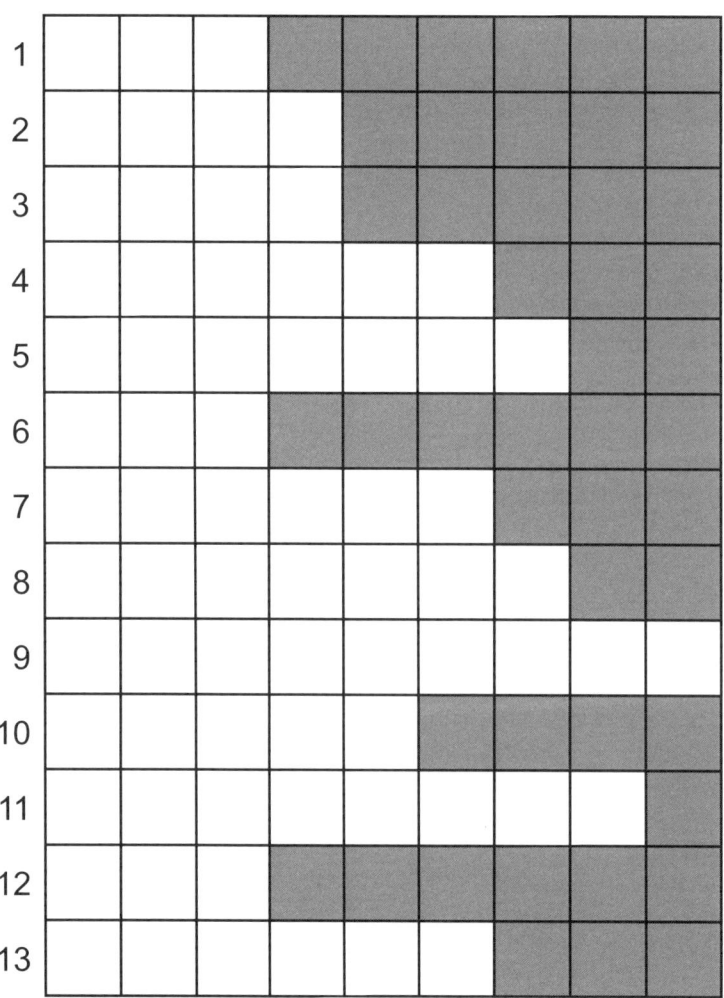

The letters in the first column spell _ _ _ _ _ _ _ _ _ _ _ _ _

Harmonious Relationships

Galatians 5:16-26

When I become a Christian, the Holy Spirit comes to live in me and my life starts to change. I experience love for God, the joy of knowing that I am forgiven and peace with God.

The next 3 characteristics of living by the Spirit deal with my relationship with other people.

Patience or long-suffering.

Read James 5:7-11.

Who are examples of patience?　　the f.......................... (v.7)

the p....................................... (v.10)

J............. (v.11)

Using the above verses, how should we demonstrate patience towards each other?

Kindness or graciousness and gentleness.

Read Colossians 3:12-13 and 2 Samuel 9:1-13.

How do these passages help you understand what it means to be kind?

Goodness or doing good to others.

Read Galatians 6:7-10.

Does doing good come naturally? (v.9)　　☐ yes　　☐ no

Whom are we commanded to do good to?
- ☐ people we like
- ☐ only Christians
- ☑ all people

None of these 3 fruit happens naturally - they all require hard work and lots and lots of practice.

To discover an important message, find the 11 words listed at the side of the word search. The words read in a straight line and can read in any direction. No letter is used more than once.

J	U	E	C	N	E	I	T	A	P	S	F
T	K	A	F	R	U	I	T	S	A	S	A
S	T	I	R	E	C	A	E	P	S	E	I
S	E	S	N	E	F	R	U	E	I	T	T
E	G	R	V	D	O	W	N	S	T	S	H
N	L	O	O	W	N	E	L	Y	I	A	F
D	L	N	D	S	L	E	T	E	R	A	U
O	D	I	L	T	Y	S	S	O	I	S	L
O	H	O	N	U	L	J	D	S	P	T	N
G	H	E	E	S	P	O	I	R	S	I	E
T	G	U	A	L	F	Y	R	U	I	T	S
S	E	L	F	C	O	N	T	R	O	L	S

FAITHFULNESS
FRUIT
GENTLENESS
GOODNESS
JOY
KINDNESS
LOVE
PATIENCE
PEACE
SELF-CONTROL
SPIRIT

Now, starting from the top and reading from left to right, write down the letters which are left in order in the spaces below.

JUST AS A TREE'S FRUIT GROWS SLOWLY

AND STEADILY, SO SHOULD THE

SPIRITUAL FRUIT.

WEEK 6
Control of the Sinful Nature

Preparation:
Read Galatians 5:16-26, Joshua 24:14, 3 John 2-8, Colossians 3:12-14, Titus 2:11-14, 1 Peter 3:15-16

Lesson Aim:
To understand what is means to 'live by the Spirit'.

Galatians
5:16-26   See notes for week 4.

Faithfulness, Gentleness, Self-control.
These 3 are primarily concerned with us.

Joshua
24:14   Faithfulness is dependability, loyalty, reliability.

3 John
v.3   Note the importance of remaining faithful to the truth (i.e. the truth of the gospel).

v.5-8   Faithfulness in showing hospitality. Our actions demonstrate the presence of the Holy Spirit in our lives.

Colossians
3:12   Gentleness is meekness, absence of arrogance. All these qualities do not just happen - they need to be put on, suggesting effort. It is these virtues that enable us to bear with one another and forgive one another (v.13-14).

1 Peter
3:15   When we tell people what we believe as Christians we need to do it with gentleness.

Titus
2:12   Self-control is the opposite of Galatians 5:19-21. We need God's grace in order to be self-controlled (v.11), but we are the ones who have to say 'no' to all ungodliness and worldly passions.

Prepare a series of cards, each one containing one thing that can be controlled by a person or by God, such as a horse, a car, the weather, your temper, a class of children, a football game, a tennis match. Prepare the same number of apples as cards, (see diagram), and write a number from 1 to 4 on the back of each one. Divide the children into 2 teams and place the apples, number side down, on the table. The teams take it in turn to pick a card and state who controls the item written on it. Then they pick an apple and are credited with the number of points written on the back. The winning team is the one to collect most points. Discuss with the children the items that are most difficult to control, such as our tempers. In today's Bible study we will see who can help us control our tempers.

Teach the Bible passage using the activity pages to help you. Revise the memory verse. Review the series with a quiz, using the apples from the introductory activity as a method of scoring.

Photocopy pages 28 and 29 for each child and add to the back of the activity book. The activity book may be taken home at the end of this session.

Control of the Sinful Nature
Galatians 5:16-26

The final 3 characteristics that should be seen in the life of the person, who is living by the Spirit, are concerned with the individual.

Faithfulness or dependability, loyalty, reliability.

Read Joshua 24:14 and 3 John:2-8.

What am I to be faithful to?

How do I show faithfulness in my life?

Gentleness or meekness and absence of arrogance.

Read Colossians 3:12-14 and 1 Peter 3:15-16.

Is it easy to be gentle?

How do these verses help me when I want to tell other people about Jesus?

Self-control

Read Titius 2:11-14.

Can we avoid the acts of the sinful nature in our own strength?

☐ yes

☐ no

We need God's g........................ to help us - but **we** are the ones who have to say, 'No!'

28

Read Galatians 5:24-26.

Paul tells the Galatian Christians they must do 3 things:

* wage war against the s.................. n.................. (v.24)

* allow the H............... S.................... to control every aspect of their lives (v.25)

* not think themselves better than other p.................. (v.26)

Then they will demonstrate the fruit of the Spirit in their lives.

Can you put the fruit in order to give your memory verse?

Write the numbers on the leaves in the correct order in the boxes below.

☐ ☐ ☐ ☐ ☐ ☐ ☐ ☐ ☐

Galatians 5:22-23

Thank God for sending his Holy Spirit to live in all believers. Ask him to help you demonstrate the fruit of the Spirit in your life.

WEEK 7
The Existence of God

Preparation:
See lesson notes for relevant Bible passages.

Lesson Aim:
To learn some of the reasons why we believe God exists.

As with all the apologetics style lessons the teacher's preparation is crucial. These notes are designed to give you some idea about how to approach the subject, and the kind of information it would be useful to have at your fingertips during the lesson. How exactly you teach the lesson is up to you. The larger and younger the class, the more structured the lesson will need to be. This is not meant to be a complete information pack. Without reading at least some of the source material for yourself the arguments will sound thin and unconvincing and you will be easily stumped by the children's questions.

INTRODUCTION

Take a transparent plastic box with lid and place some lego in it. Give it a good shake to make a motor-bike. Give it a bigger shake. Can we make a motor-bike? So did we come about with just a big shake? Let's see what the Bible has to say?

Make a chart (get the children to give you the answers)

Answers tend to fall into these kinds of categories with both adults and children (with a few wild ones thrown in). The answers will not be as clearly articulated as the ones here so you may need to question further to understand clearly the answer being given.

It is suggested you look at the evidence under the following headings:

1. What does science say about God? (Covers science has disproved God and design and beauty in creation arguments.)

2. Have we seen God in Jesus? (Covers the evidence for God's existence via Jesus and no-one has seen God arguments.)

3. Can we rely on experience? (Covers the remaining arguments.)

Any other questions can be discussed if there is time.

Why do you (or some people) think God exists?	Why do some people say that God does not exist?
Design and beauty in creation.	Science has disproved religion.
Evidence via Jesus.	No one can see God so he's probably not there.
Experience of God.	No experience of God.
Family believes.	Family does not believe.

1. WHAT DOES SCIENCE SAY ABOUT GOD?

Reading: 'Does God Play Dice?' by John Houghton (IVP)

'Darwin on Trial' by Phillip Johnson (IVP)

This section is the most difficult for a non-scientist to teach but it is an area where most children's faith is very much under attack from teachers and from other children. It is consequently the area where they have the most questions.

For thousands of years people looked at creation in all its vastness, beauty and complexity and could not understand how it could have come about if God had not made it. Judaism and Christianity look to the story in Genesis 1 about how God created the heavens and the earth. Other world religions have their own stories about how their god or gods brought this about.

When science started to answer some of the questions about how the earth came into existence, people started to think of God as only being involved in the steps of creation not explained by science (a God of the gaps).

As science progressed and explained more and more about how our world came into being, the gaps in our knowledge got smaller and people started to conclude that God's role in creation had been, or soon would be, explained away. This became a good excuse to deny that God existed at all. Christians and others who refused to give up the idea that God created all things were seen as old fashioned and unreasonable.

HOW DO PEOPLE TODAY THINK OUR WORLD CAME INTO BEING?

The theory most children will have been taught at school is that the universe spontaneously came into being at a point in time, the Big Bang Theory.

The Big Bang Theory (made very simple indeed!) A fuller and relatively easy to understand account of this can be found in the first two chapters of John Houghton's book.

Before the universe was formed all that existed was a very dense collection of 'matter' (from which atoms are made) and empty space. The matter was much more dense that anything that we know in our world. In fact an area of this matter the size of a cricket ball would weigh a million tons!

This ball of matter exploded and all the particles started to move away from each other.

Some of the particles were attracted together to form various kinds of atoms. In turn, these atoms were attracted towards each other and eventually formed stars. The planets in our solar system were probably formed about 4.5 billion years ago from the debris released from a second explosion in our sun.

There is quite convincing evidence that an event like this marked the beginning of things. The Big Bang theory explains many of the phenomena we can observe in the universe, e.g. the universe is still rapidly expanding. The most distant galaxies we can observe are moving away from us at 200,000 km per second. But does this theory explain away the need for a creator God?

The amount of energy involved in the explosion had to be very precise. If the collection of matter had exploded with fractionally too much energy all the particles would have been blown apart with such velocity that they would not have been attracted to form atoms and thus stars and planets. If there had been fractionally too little energy, the attraction between the 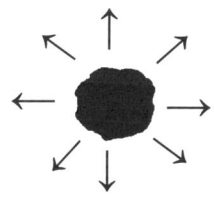 particles would have been so strong that they would have reverted to the state they were in before the explosion. Either way the universe would not have been formed.

Increasingly, scientists studying this model of the universe are impressed by the fact that the universe appears to be exceedingly fine-tuned in the sense that its forces have to be balanced to an incredible degree of accuracy in order for life to be possible. The physicist Paul Davies stated that the accuracy required here is the same as that needed by a marksman in order to hit a target 1" square from the other end of the universe (20 billion light years away). His conclusion is that 'the impression of design is overwhelming.' This squares with the biblical claim that the universe was designed.

HOW DO PEOPLE TODAY THINK THAT LIFE AROSE?

The Urey-Miller experiment, carried out in 1953, passed an electrical charge simulating lightning through a pre-biotic soup, causing it to form some amino acids. Amino acids are the basic building blocks of DNA. Some scientists suggested that this experiment demonstrated how life on earth evolved. Before life arose on earth, the atoms necessary to make a living cell were already present. As time went on some of these atoms joined up to form molecules.

The energy needed for this to happen came from the sun and the process was aided by gases present in the atmosphere at that time, e.g. ammonia.

One day, somewhere on the earth all these molecules happened to be in exactly the right places in relation to each other to join together and make the complex molecules necessary for life in its simplest form to evolve spontaneously. Again the sun provided the energy necessary for these chemical reactions. David Attenborough, in his book 'Life on Earth', explains this process and makes it seem quite plausible (chapter 1).

The DNA in the cell nucleus contains the genetic information required for specifying the proteins and it is exceedingly complex in the sense that the amino acids have got to be in the right order. Getting the building blocks is one thing, getting them in the right order is totally different. This is why Sir Fred Hoyle stated that the probability of life arising by chance is about the same as that of a typhoon blowing through a junk yard and forming a Boeing 747.

Many of the children will be taught the theory of evolution as fact at school. When discussing evolution it is helpful to distinguish between micro- and macro-evolution. Micro-evolution consists of minor variations within limits through natural selection, e.g. the change in length of finch beaks which Darwin observed. This is not controversial. But the mechanism that explains how things vary does not explain how they came to exist in the first place. Macro-evolution, on the other hand, is about the development of the living cell from non-living materials, of multicellular from single-celled structures, of new body plans, new organs, etc., and this is much more controversial.

As science has progressed and appears to answer more and more questions about how the world functions, some people have concluded that God's role in it all is superfluous. But understanding how something works does not preclude the idea of someone having designed it. If we consider a Ford motor car we can see how flawed that logic is. Motor mechanics understand exactly how the car works, but this is not an argument about the existence of a Mr Ford who designed it. The more intricate we discover the universe to be, the more it should take us back to worship the designer who created it.

Christians are not able to say for certain whether the universe was formed via the Big Bang, or whether a form of evolution took place. These are not questions the Bible answers directly. What we can say with certainty from the Bible is that God caused it to happen - and the scientific evidence backs us all the way!

2. HAVE WE SEEN GOD IN JESUS?
Reading: 'A Fresh Start' by John Chapman (St Matthias Press) chapters 6-8.

'The Day Death Died' by Michael Green (Evidence for the Resurrection) (IVP).

Has anyone ever seen God?
Either, throw a sheet over someone not known to the group. Ask the children to offer suggestions as to what the person is like, e.g. red hair, curly hair, blue eyes, kind, thoughtful, etc. They do not know what the person is really like until you take the sheet away.

Or, hold up a covered photo of a famous person. Uncover the photo and discuss what the children know about this person. Point out that we will only really get to know the person by listening to what they say and watching what they do.

So how can we get to know God? Has anyone ever seen him? The answer to this question is no, but this is not all the Bible has to say about the matter.

No-one has ever seen God, but Jesus, who is God, has made him known.
John 1:18

The Bible seems to suggest that, by looking at Jesus and listening to his teaching, we can know God.

How do we know that this is true?
Jesus did not arrive from heaven out of the blue. The Old Testament scriptures had foretold his coming. He was 'long awaited'. He was not quite what religious men of the times had expected, but that was due to their misunderstanding of what the Old Testament scriptures taught about him.

Jesus left his disciples in no doubt that to know him was to know God.

Philip said, 'Show us the Father and that will be enough for us.' Jesus answered, 'Don't you know me Philip, even after I have been among you such a long time? Anyone who has seen me has seen the Father. How can you say 'show us the Father'? Don't you believe that I am in the Father and the Father is in me?'
John 14:8-10

Although we have not seen God, mankind has in Jesus. The record of what he did and said are in the Bible. These statements cannot be accepted until we answer two further questions.

Was Jesus telling the truth when he made these claims?

Do we really have accurate records of what he said in the Bible?

The second question is the subject of a different lesson in which we will establish beyond all reasonable doubt that the Bible is entirely trustworthy concerning the things about which it speaks. (Year 1, Book 2, week 6 'Can we rely on the New Testament?') We will discover that what we have in today's versions is what was written down by the Bible writers in the first century. For the purpose of this lesson we will assume the Bible's accuracy.

How do we know that Jesus was God?
a. He claimed to be God.

b. His actions were consistent with his claims.

c. He was resurrected and never died again.

(a) Jesus claimed to be God.
These claims were made both privately and publicly. The following are just some of his claims.

> **I am the bread of life** (John 6:35) - claiming that in him people would find satisfaction for ever.
>
> **I am the light of the world** (John 8:12) - claiming to have all understanding and to be the source of all knowledge.
>
> **I am the way, the truth and the life** (John 14:6) - an exclusive claim to be the only way to God, the ultimate truth and the giver of eternal life.
>
> **The judge of all the world**
> (Matthew 25:31ff).
>
> **Lord and God** (John 8:56-58) - 'Before Abraham was I Am' - Jesus uses the Old Testament name of God, 'I Am' (e.g. Exodus 3:14), for himself.

There is really no doubt about who Jesus claimed to be, yet when you ask people who are not Christians who they think Jesus was, they will usually say he was a 'good man' or a 'great teacher'. But surely a person making such outrageous claims can hardly be regarded as a 'good man'.

Regarding this conclusion C.S. Lewis wrote,

> *'A man who was merely a man and said the sort of things Jesus said would not be a great moral teacher, he would be a lunatic - on a level with the man who says he is a poached egg - or else he would be the Devil of Hell.'*
> *'Let us not come with any patronising nonsense about his being a great human teacher. He has not left that open to us. He did not intend to.'*
> (from 'Mere Christianity')

We are left with 3 options; either his claims are true and he is who he claimed to be, **the Son of God**, i.e. God himself in human form, or his claims are false. If the latter, he is either a **madman** who just thinks he is God (there are plenty of patients in mental institutions who have such delusions) or an **evil man**, who knowingly deceived his followers or colluded with them in order to gain popularity, money or power. Let's deal with these two alternatives in turn.

Madman. There is no evidence that Jesus was in any way psychologically disturbed. Mad people who make such claims always exhibit other evidence of severely disordered thought. The recorded words of Jesus do not suggest any such mental disorder.

Evil man. If he had simply been a con-man it is difficult to explain why Jesus should have been willing to die rather that admit that he was a fraud. The gospel writers are unanimous in portraying Jesus as one who chose quite deliberately to die (Mark 8:31; 9:31; 10:33) and made no attempt to take opportunities to save himself (Mark 15:4). It is even more difficult to explain how a mere con-man could possibly have contrived to have himself raised from the dead.

Some have suggested that Jesus was **demon-possessed** (e.g. Mark 3:22-27). This might explain some of his power but does not square with his keenness to exorcise, or his statements about the purpose of his life and death and his moral goodness. (e.g. Matthew 4:10, Mark 3:27, Luke 10:17-18; 13:16; 22:31).

(b) Jesus' actions were consistent with his claims

Jesus' character
The things Jesus said and did were always consistent with him being God. He was loving, patient and people-centred, but also just and judgmental with penetrating insight. Even his closest companions were willing to vouch for his perfection (e.g. 1 John 1:2). Would your friends say this of you?

The miracles
Jesus seemed to be able to do all the things that you might expect a creator God to be able to do. He could change the weather (Mark 4:35-41). He could restore good health or even life (Mark 5:21-43). He could recreate unseeing eyes (John 9) and demonstrated complete control over spiritual powers (e.g. Mark 9:14-28).

(c) Jesus was resurrected and never died again
Jesus rose from the dead as he predicted he would. He used this action to validate his other claims. It is therefore of great importance that we are certain that the resurrection actually happened. Here are just some of the reasons for believing that Jesus did in fact rise from the dead:

1. No-one ever produced the body though it would have been in the interest of both the Jews and the Romans to do so.

2. Many saw him alive - over 500 people at one time according to Paul in 1 Corinthians 15:5-8, many of whom were still alive at the time of his writing and could therefore be checked with.

3. The disciples never changed their story though many of them died violent deaths, which they could have avoided if they had denied that Jesus was God and had risen from the dead.

4. None of the apostles changed their minds about Jesus.

3. CAN WE RELY ON EXPERIENCE?

Some people feel they experience God and therefore say God exists. Some people do not feel they experience God and therefore conclude that God does not exist. So whose experience is right and whose is wrong?

Most things that we experience are really there, but experience can play tricks on you, so you experience something which isn't there, e.g. a mirage.

Sometimes you cannot experience something that is there because your body cannot recognise it, e.g. music played to a deaf person. You may also experience something without realising it is there, e.g. a small child experiencing gravity. So experience can be an unreliable guide to truth.

Before people give their lives to God and become Christians the Bible says they are unable to understand who God is.

> *He who belongs to God hears what God says. The reason you do not hear is because you do not belong to God.*
> John 8:47

> *The God of this age has blinded the minds of unbelievers, so that they cannot see the light of the gospel of the glory of Christ who is the image of God.*
> 2 Corinthians 4:4

> *As for you - you were dead in your transgressions and sins in which you used to live when you followed the ways of this world.*
> Ephesians 2:1

So part of the reason why people who are not Christians do not experience God is because their sins have made them deaf, blind and dead and therefore unable to understand that he is there.

However, some of their lack of experience is due to ignorance (like not knowing about gravity). This is why explaining to others what we believe and why is very important. It goes hand in hand with praying to God that he would allow them to see him despite their sin.

Talk about 3 characters walking along a wall:-

    faith in the middle

    facts in front

    feelings behind.

When they all keep their eyes to the front they are alright, but when they start to look behind them they begin to wobble all over the place. Draw out the analogy that if we just rely on our feelings to say whether or not God exists, that will let us down because our feelings are unreliable and fluctuate. We need faith, based on the facts of Jesus' words and actions, to establish us in our Christian lives.

CONCLUSION

Refer back to the chart made at the beginning of the lesson.

Look at the different categories and briefly recapitulate on the arguments.

Conclude by showing that there is more evidence **for** the existence of God than against.

How God Should Be Worshipped

Week 8 — **THE TABERNACLE** — *Exodus 35:1 - 40:38*
To understand that worship that is acceptable to God is worship carried out according to his decrees.

Week 9 — **SACRIFICE** — *Leviticus 1:1 - 5:19; 16:1-34*
To understand that sin has to be dealt with before we can worship a holy God.

Week 10 — **FEASTS** — *Leviticus 23:1-44, Matthew 26:17-30*
To learn the importance of regular times of remembering what God has done for his people.

Week 11 — **THE NEW COVENANT** — *Hebrews 8:1 - 10:14*
To understand why the death of Jesus makes it possible for us to approach a holy God.

Week 12 — **DAILY LIFE** — *Hebrews 10:19-31*
To learn how we should worship God today.

 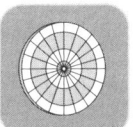

To understand how God wants us to worship him.

When God made the first man, Adam, he chose to have a friendship with him. God talked with him, revealed himself to him, gave him a job to do and gave him a rule to keep. When Adam and Eve rebelled against God, breaking the rule that God had given them, they became sinful. Since God is perfect he could not live in fellowship with them anymore and he banished them from his presence (the garden). All the children descended from Adam and Eve were born rebels. No-one was fit to live with God.

Later in the book of Genesis we read about something very remarkable. God made a promise to Abraham, an ordinary sinful man, one not fit to be in his presence. God promised that Abraham and his descendants would be God's special people and he would be their God. Could it be that God was prepared to ignore Abraham's sinful nature in order to be friends with him? We know that God **cannot** do that. So how **could** a holy God make that promise to a sinful man?

About 450 years later the descendants of Abraham's grandson, Jacob (later named Israel), became slaves in the land of Egypt. Because of his promise to Abraham, God rescued the Israelites and led them out of Egypt into the desert. There he showed Moses how the Israelites should behave as God's people. He also showed them how they could arrange things so that a holy God could live among them despite their sin.

In this series we will be looking at these instructions for worship that were given to Moses. We will see that worship was not something a person decided to do for God. When people worshipped God they were following the instructions that God had given them! In this way God could accept them as his people, despite their sinfulness, and live among them as their God. The last 2 studies look at the way Jesus Christ completely fulfilled the requirements of the Law and the difference this makes to the way we worship God

Let us be thankful, and so worship God acceptably with reverence and awe.

Hebrews 12:28

LET US BE THANKFUL, AND SO WORSHIP GOD ACCEPTABLY WITH REVERENCE AND AWE.

Hebrews 12:28

WEEK 8
The Tabernacle

Preparation:
Read Exodus 35:1 – 40:38, using the Bible Study notes to help you.

Lesson Aim:
To understand that worship that is acceptable to God is worship carried out according to his decrees.

The teacher needs to read the whole of these chapters to get a proper overview of the instructions God gave to Moses regarding the Tabernacle, but only some of it will be studied with the children.

35:7 Sea cows are also known as dugongs.

35:9 The ephod and breast piece were worn by the High Priest. The ephod was a linen garment worn over the tunic. It was richly embroidered and on the front of it was a pouch, which was covered with jewels. The pouch contained 2 lots, which allowed the priest to determine the will of God. (See notes for Life in Bible Times (Dwellings), Book 2 Week 1.) For a detailed description of the ephod and breast piece see Exodus 39:2-21.

35:22 The wave offering was a contribution offering. (See also Leviticus 7:28-31.)

36:15 A cubit was the distance between the elbow and the tip of the middle finger.

36:20-30 The coverings of the Tabernacle were supported on wooden frames. These frames made a rectangular structure, 30 cubits long and 10 cubits wide.

36:35-38 There were 2 curtains - one separating the Most Holy Place from the Holy Place and one at the entrance to the Tabernacle (see 26:31-37). The Most Holy Place (or Holy of Holies) was the inner room and measured 10 cubits square. The curtain separating the Most Holy Place from the Holy Place served 2 purposes. First, it acted as a visible barrier between a holy God and sinful people. The cherubim woven into the curtain were a reminder of the cherubim at the gate of Eden, preventing Adam and Eve's return. Second, by separating off the Most Holy Place it allowed the priests to enter the Holy Place to offer worship to God.

37:1-5 The Ark was a wooden box, covered with gold. It contained the stone tablets, on which were written the 10 commandments (40:20), reminding the Israelites that they were living under God's rule.

37:6-9 The atonement cover, (or mercy seat), was thought of as God's throne. It was the place where God would meet with Moses and issue his decrees (25:22). The Ark was placed in the Most Holy Place and no-one was allowed to enter apart from the High Priest on the Day of Atonement (see notes for Week 9).

37:10-16 The table was situated on the north wall of the Holy Place (40:22). On it were 12 loaves of bread, one for each of the 12 tribes of Israel (25:30). The priests replaced the bread each week, eating the old loaves as a meal in God's presence (Leviticus 24:5-9).

37:17-24 The lampstand was the only source of light in the Tabernacle and was kept burning continuously (Leviticus 24:1-4). The lampstand was placed on the south side of the Tabernacle (Exodus 40:24).

37:24 A talent was the equivalent of 300 shekels and weighed approximately 75 pounds (34 kilograms).

37:25-29 The Altar of Incense was placed in front of the curtain separating the Most Holy Place from the Holy Place (30:6; 40:26-28). The priest, as the people's representative, offered incense twice a day on the altar as a symbol of the people's prayers (Luke 1:8-10).

38:1-7   The Altar of Burnt Offering was sited in front of the entrance to the Tabernacle and was the first thing the people would see when they entered the courtyard (40:6). It was a reminder that atonement for sin was needed before people could approach a holy God.

38:8   The basin was placed between the Altar of Burnt Offering and the entrance to the Tabernacle. The priests washed their hands and feet in it to purify themselves before entering the Tabernacle (30:17-21).

Ask for 3 volunteers. Pretend to be a waiter and offer child 1 a breakfast menu. Child 1 chooses from the menu. The waiter goes to get the order and returns, bringing more than was ordered. (Use pictures or play food.) The waiter tries to convince the child that this is better than what was ordered.

Do the same with child 2, but bring back less than he ordered. Try to convince the child that what the waiter has brought is adequate.

Repeat the procedure with child 3, but bring something entirely different from the order. Try to convince the child that this is so much better.

Discuss what is going wrong. Point out that people often think that worshipping God is like that. God has told us what he wants, but we try to give him more or less than he wants, or something entirely different. Do they think that God is pleased with worship he has not asked for?

In this series we are going to study what God asked the Israelites to do to worship him and how that affects the way we should worship him today. We will find out that it was really important for the Israelites to do exactly what God said, because that was the only way they could please him and be part of his family.

Tell the children that the first thing they will look at is the Tabernacle, the special tent where God's people went to worship him. Show them where in the Bible God's instructions about the tent can be found. Use the activity pages to help teach the lesson. Do not get bogged down in too much detail; the children should have the big picture of the tabernacle and contents, and need to understand that everything was done according to God's plan, not Moses'. Teach the memory verse.

It is helpful to have pictures of the Tabernacle and its furnishings (see activity pages). Also, some Christian bookshops sell books containing a model made from card for home assembly.

The activity pages are very detailed, so that they can be kept as a reference for future use. Photocopy page 39 on coloured card and pages 40-46 on paper for each child. Each child also requires an A4 sheet of the same coloured card to be a back cover and an A4 slide binder. Pages 39-45 form part of the book, whereas page 46 is left separate. The children cut out the pieces of the tabernacle from page 46 and glue them onto the plan on page 45 as you talk about them during the lesson. (For ease of handling, the items of furniture are twice as big as they would be if they were to scale with the Tabernacle and courtyard.) Keep the activity books at church until the end of the series.

God Tells How He Should Be

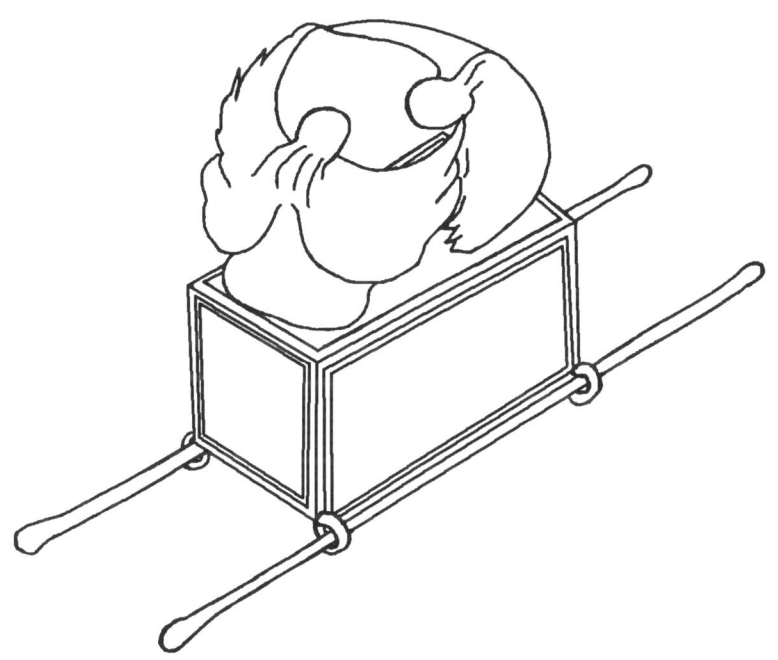

Worshipped

God Tells How He Should Be Worshipped

When God made the first man - Adam - he chose to have a friendship with him. God talked to him, revealed himself to him, gave him a job to do and gave him a rule to keep. When Adam and Eve rebelled against God, breaking the rule that God had given them, they became sinful. Since God is perfect, he could not live in fellowship with them anymore and he banished them from his presence (the garden). All the children descended from Adam and Eve were born rebels. No-one was fit to live with God.

Later in the book of Genesis we read about something very remarkable. God made a promise to a man called Abraham, an ordinary, sinful man, one not fit to be in his presence. God promised that Abraham and his descendants would be God's special people and he would be their God. Could it be that God was prepared to ignore Abraham's sinful nature in order to be friends with him? NO! We know that God cannot do that. So how could a holy God make that promise to a sinful man?

About 450 years later the descendants of Abraham's grandson, Jacob (also called Israel), had become slaves in the land of Egypt. Because of his promise to Abraham, God rescued the Israelites and led them into the desert. There he showed Moses how the Israelites should behave as God's people. He also showed them how they could arrange things so that a holy God could live among them, despite their sin.

In this series we will be looking at these instructions for worship that God gave to Moses. We will see that worship was not something a person decided to do for God. When people worshipped God they were following the instructions that God had given them. In this way God could accept them as his people, despite their sinfulness, and live among them as their God.

The Tabernacle

Exodus 35 - 40

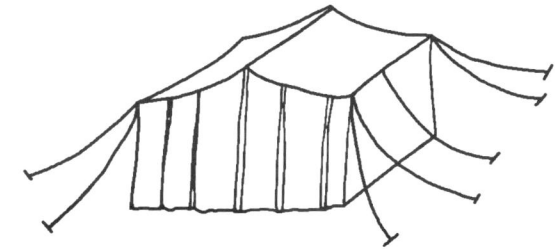

God told Moses to build a Tabernacle, a special kind of tent, where God could live among his people. He told Moses to put it right in the middle of the Israelites' camp.

The Tabernacle was made in such a way that it could be easily taken down, carried to a different place and put up again. Other people's so-called gods lived in one place and, if you wanted to worship them, you had to travel to that place. But God was not like that. He lived with his chosen people, wherever they were.

On M................ S.................. God spoke to M............... (Exodus 34:29). God gave him very detailed instructions about how to make the Tabernacle. Everything had to be done exactly as God said. Only then could God live with his people.

In Exodus 35:4-29 Moses gave the people a huge list of all the things that would be needed to build the Tabernacle.

Name 5 of the things that were needed.

....
....
....
....
....

Where were these things to come from? (35:21)

....

Who was to do the work? (35:10)

....

Read chapter 36:2-7. Why did Moses tell the people to stop bringing their gifts? He could have made the Tabernacle bigger and grander. Why was it important to keep to the instructions?

The Tabernacle

The Israelites made the Tabernacle (or Tent of Meeting, as it is sometimes called) according to God's instructions. The skeleton of the tent was made from wooden frames. Each one slotted into two silver bases, which held it upright. The inside of the Tabernacle was lined with purple, blue and scarlet curtains. These curtains had creatures with wings, called cherubim, sewn into them as part of the God-given design. The curtains were all joined together with golden clasps. A large curtain divided the Tabernacle into two rooms. The room nearest to the entrance was called the Holy Place. The room behind the curtain was called the Most Holy Place, or the Holy of Holies. God would be present in this room in a very special way.

The Tabernacle had three coverings over it (36:14-19).

The first covering was made from ....

Over that was a covering of ....

The outermost covering was made from ....

The Courtyard (38:9-13)

God told Moses to make a courtyard around the outside of the Tabernacle. The courtyard walls were made of linen curtains, supported by posts set into bronze bases. Both the Tabernacle and the courtyard were tied down with ropes and tent pegs.

The north side of the courtyard was .... cubits long.
The south side of the courtyard was .... cubits long.
The west side of the courtyard was .... cubits long.
The entrance to the courtyard was on the east side.   ← 1 cubit →
The entrance was covered by curtains made of linen,
with blue, scarlet and purple yarn.

The Contents of the Tabernacle

The Ark of the Covenant was a wooden chest covered with gold, inside and out. It had a foot at each corner. Attached to each foot was a gold ring. Two poles, also covered with gold, were slotted through the rings on either side. This meant that the Ark could be moved from place to place without anyone touching it. The Ark had a cover made of pure gold with two cherubim on it. It was called the atonement cover. Moses put the stone tablets, on which were written the ten commandments, inside the Ark.

Read 37:1-5 and fill in the measurements of the Ark.

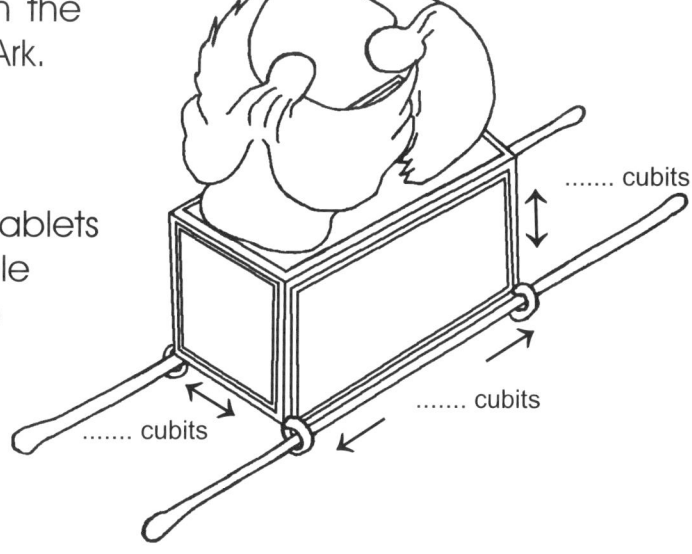

.... cubits
.... cubits
.... cubits

Since the Ark contained the tablets of the Law, it reminded people of God's rule over them. The cover with its cherubim was thought of as God's throne. The Ark was placed behind the curtain in the Most Holy Place.

In the Holy Place were the following items:

The Table was made of acacia wood, covered with gold. It had a ring at each corner and poles for carrying it around (37:10-16). On the table were twelve loaves of bread, which were replaced every Sabbath.

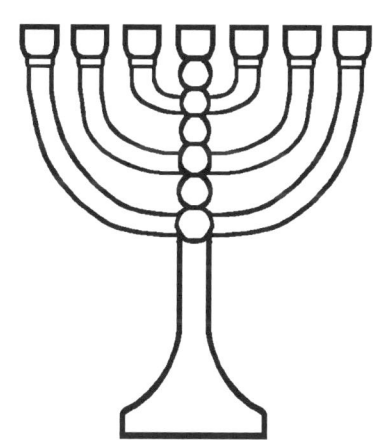

The Lampstand was made from pure gold. It carried seven lamps and was decorated with almond flowers and buds made from gold (37:17-24). It took .... of gold to make the lampstand (37:24).

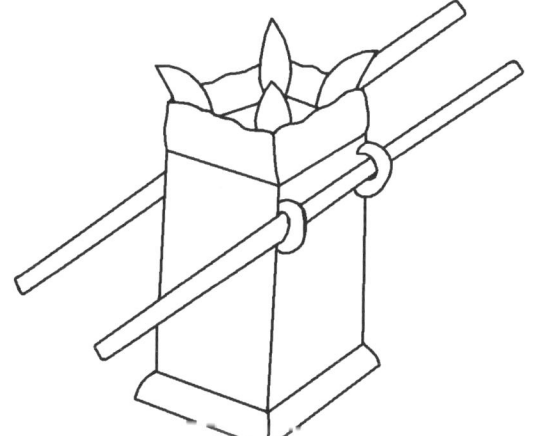

The Altar of Incense also had rings at each corner and poles to carry it around. It had horns at each corner and was covered with gold (37:25-28).

In the courtyard were the following:

The Altar of Burnt Offering was much bigger than the altar of incense. It too was made of wood with rings, poles and horns, but this time covered with bronze (38:1-7). All the tools used with this altar were made from bronze.

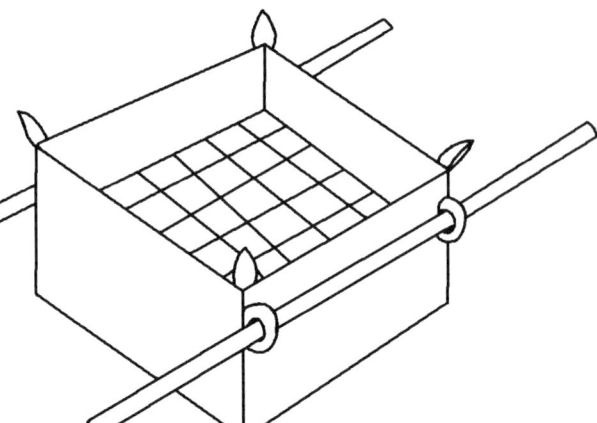

A bronze basin was made for the priests to wash their hands and feet before entering the Tabernacle (38:8).

When everything had been put in its proper place, Moses anointed the Tabernacle and everything in it so that it would be holy - set apart for the worship of God. Aaron and his sons, who were to serve in the Tabernacle as priests, were also anointed.

How do we know that this was done in a way which was acceptable to God? (40:34-35)

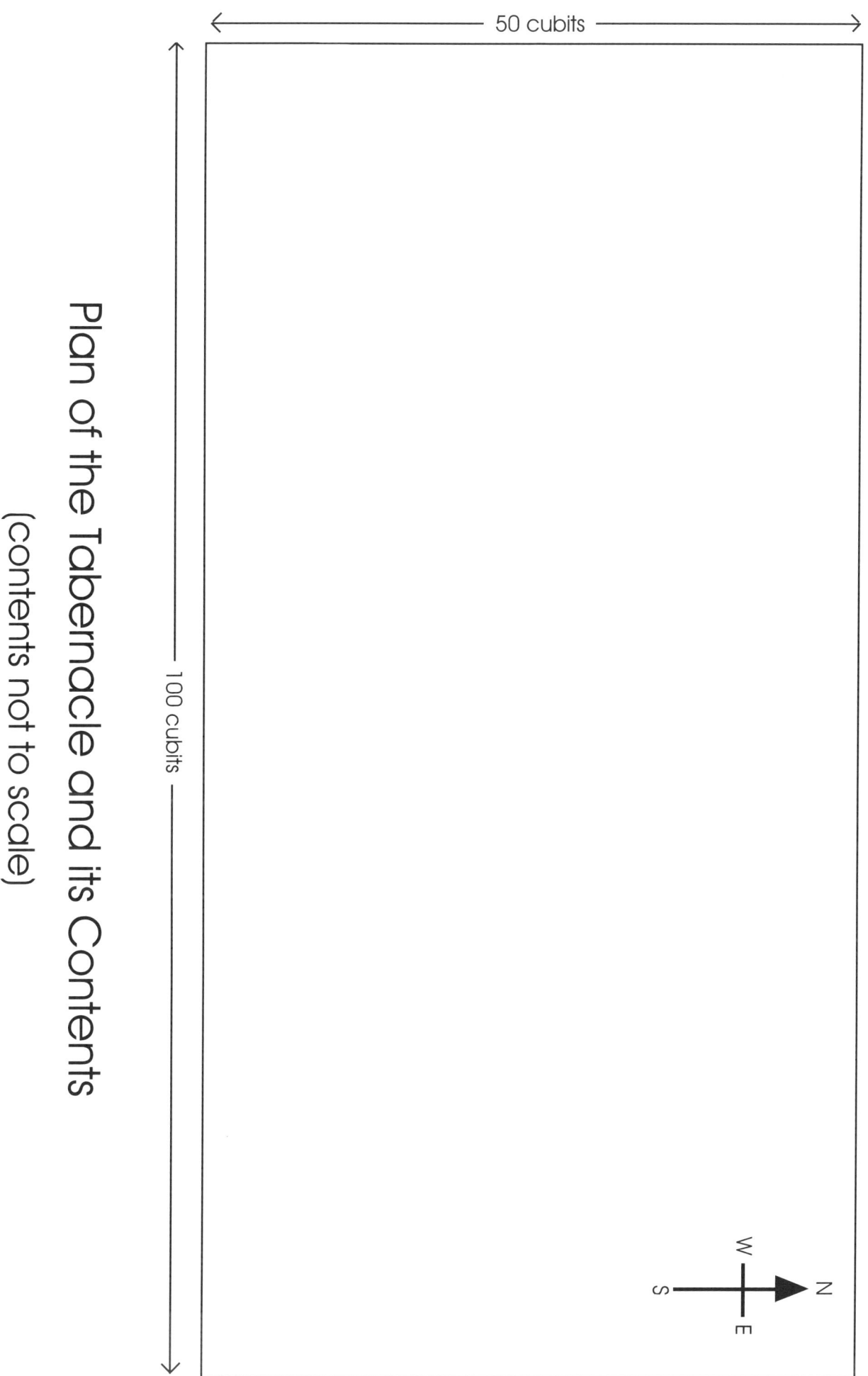

The Tabernacle and contents - to cut out and glue onto the courtyard.

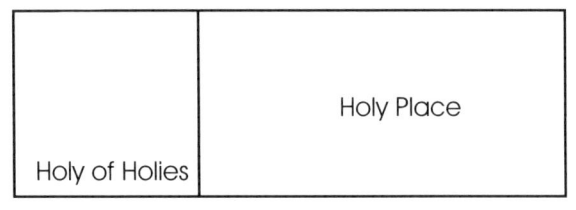

The Tabernacle was sited at the west end of the courtyard, with the opening facing east.

The Ark of the Covenant goes in the Holy of Holies.

The Altar of Incense was placed directly opposite the Ark, in the Holy Place, separated by the curtain.

The table was on the north wall of the Holy Place.

The lampstand was on the south wall of the Holy Place.

The Altar of Burnt Offering was placed before the entrance to the Tabernacle. The basin was placed between the entrance to the Tabernacle and the Altar of Burnt Offering.

The Tabernacle is to scale with the courtyard. All the contents are double their size.

WEEK 9
Sacrifice

Preparation:
Read Leviticus 1:1 - 5:19; 16:1-34, using the Bible Study notes to help you.

Lesson Aim:
To understand that sin has to be dealt with before we can worship a holy God.

This lesson looks at what the Israelites had to do if God was going to live among his people. They had the Tabernacle set up in the middle of the camp, which showed that God had come to live with his people, just as he had promised. However, the Israelites were still not able to be in God's presence. The Most Holy Place, with the Ark of the Covenant, the place where a person could really meet with God, was screened off with a big curtain. No one was allowed in apart from the High Priest on the Day of Atonement.

On one hand the Tabernacle seemed to be teaching the Israelites that God could now live with them, on the other hand the curtain acted as a huge 'no entry' sign.

In the book of Leviticus we read the instructions God gave to Moses about the various things the Israelites had to do if God was to live among them. This study looks at the sacrificial system; next week looks at the Feasts.

1:3   Burnt offerings were a way of saying thank-you to God - perhaps for having been saved from disaster or for a successful journey. They could also be made in order to ask God what to do in the future. Sometimes the worshipper just wanted to thank God that he was one of the chosen people. These offerings were completely burnt on the altar. Note the emphasis on 'the best'. The worshipper could not bring any old animal to offer to God. Male was considered to be more important than female and the animal had to be without defect (cf. Malachi 1:6-14).

1:5   The animal was slaughtered by the worshipper, not by the priest.

1:14   The worshipper brought what he could afford. Those who could not afford a bull or a sheep or goat brought a bird.

1:15   Note that the blood of the bird is drained out on the side of the altar. There was not enough blood to splash it on all 4 sides of the altar, as was done when the larger animals were sacrificed.

2:1   Grain offerings were also gift offerings (like the burnt offerings). Each year the 'first fruits' of the crops were given as a grain offering to say thank-you to God for the harvest.

2:11   Note the prohibition on the use of leaven (yeast) and honey. This may have been because they were liable to 'go off'.

2:13   Salt was a preservative.

3:1   Fellowship offerings, sometimes called peace offerings, were similar to the burnt offerings. However, instead of the whole animal being burnt, only the fat and some of the inner parts were burnt on the altar. The rest was eaten as a fellowship meal and was shared by the worshippers and the priests. This fellowship meal was a way of remembering the peace between God and his chosen people.

4:3   The sin offering was instituted to deal with unintentional sin (4:2). It differed from the burnt offering in the way in which the blood was dealt with and in how the animal was burnt.

5:15   The guilt offering was also offered in the case of unintentional sin. It is not clear which sins required the sin offering and which the guilt offering.

16:1-34   The Day of Atonement. It seemed that even the constant sacrifices of animals on the people's behalf could not stop the Tabernacle becoming tarnished with their sin. So once a year the High Priest had to carry out a special ceremony to make the Tabernacle clean again.

16:13   This verse seems to suggest that if the High Priest looked on the atonement cover he would die. By the time of Jesus the High Priest went into the Most Holy Place with a rope tied round his ankle, so that if he was struck dead he could be pulled out again.

Discuss the entry requirements for different activities. Examples are: height restrictions for certain theme park rides and swimming pool slides (usually need to be taller than 1m or 1m 20), good eyesight in order to drive a car or an aeroplane, special qualifications to practise as a doctor, dentist, etc., a ticket to travel on a train or bus. Ask the children, 'What do you need to be able to …?' List the various answers on a board. Finally ask, 'What do you need to be able to meet God face to face?' The answer you want is 'to be sinless'. Highlight the problem, then lead into the study with, 'Today we will see how God told his people to overcome this problem.'

Teach the passage, using the activity pages as a guide. It might be helpful to divide the children into small groups and give each group one of the sacrifices to research and feed back to the rest of the group. Revise the memory verse as a game, using the concept of substitution. Divide the children into teams of equal numbers. Each team requires a memory verse set, with one word of the verse and reference written on each sheet of paper, and the same number of easily transportable items as words. The transportable items can be table tennis balls, sponges, balls of newspaper, etc. Each team sits in a row, one behind the other. The shuffled set of memory verse words is placed at one end of the row and the group of transportable items at the other end. The team has to transport their items, one at a time, from hand to hand along the row and substitute them for the words of their memory verse. Only one item can move along the row at any one time. The winner is the first team to substitute all their items for the memory verse and put it in the correct order. At the end remind the children that the animal was sacrificed as a substitute for the person who had sinned.

Photocopy pages 49-52 for each child and add to the back of the activity book.

Sacrifice

Leviticus 1:1 - 5:19

In our last lesson we learned about the Tabernacle, the tent God told his people to make to be a fit place for him to live. When the Tabernacle was finished, Moses set it up in the middle of the camp. Then the cloud on the top of Mount Sinai, which had shown everyone that God was present, came down and covered the Tabernacle. God had come to live with his people, just as he had promised.

However, even though God had come to live with them, the Israelites were still not able to be in God's presence. The Most Holy Place, with the Ark of the Covenant, the place where a person could really meet with God, was screened off by a big curtain. No one was allowed in.

On the one hand the Tabernacle seemed to be teaching the Israelites that God could now live with them. On the other hand the curtain acted as a huge no entry sign.

God told Moses what the Tent of Meeting was to be used for. We can read about this in the Book of Leviticus. It was only possible for God to live with his people if they did exactly as he said.

Look through the first 5 chapters of Leviticus. How many different types of sacrifice can you find? ....

Read the instructions for the burnt offering in chapter 1 and fill in the blanks. The burnt offering could be a young bull, a sheep, a ...., a dove or a young .... If it was a bull, it had to be without .... It had to be taken to the .... of the Tent of Meeting. The person who brought it had to lay his .... on its .... so it would be accepted on his behalf to make .... for him. Then he had to kill it and the .... were to bring the .... and sprinkle it on all 4 sides of the altar. The worshipper had to skin the animal and .... it into pieces. The legs and inner parts had to be washed with .... The priests had to burn most/some/all of it on the altar.

The instructions given for the other animals that could be burnt offerings were similar to those given for a bull.

Would you say the instructions were ☐ confusing ☐ very precise
                                     ☐ quite vague ☐ not very clear

The idea of killing animals and spreading their blood about the place makes most of us feel quite ill! Why should God want this gruesome activity going on in his dwelling place?

To answer this question we need to go back to the big problem. How can a holy God promise to live with sinful people? If a sinful person came before God, God's anger at that person's sin would be so great that he could not survive. When a person brought an animal as a sacrifice to God, he laid his hand on its head. As he did this his sins were somehow transferred onto the animal. What happened to the animal after that was what the worshipper deserved because of his sin. So the worshipper could experience God without dying as a result. If you were one of those early Israelites, you would have understood how serious your sin was, as you watched an animal being killed instead of you.

There were three main types of sacrifice.

1. Gift Sacrifices

Burnt Offerings were a way of saying thank you to God, perhaps for having been saved from disaster, or having had a successful journey. On other occasions sacrifices were made in order to ask God what to do in the future. Sometimes the worshipper just wanted to thank God that he was one of the chosen people. These gift offerings would be completely burnt on the altar.

Grain Offerings were also gift offerings. Each year the 'first fruits' of the crops would be given as a grain offering, to say thank you to God for a successful harvest.

2. Fellowship Offerings

These offerings, sometimes called peace offerings, were similar to burnt offerings. However, instead of the whole animal being burnt, only the animal's fat and some of its inner parts were burned on the altar. The rest was eaten in a fellowship meal, shared by the worshippers and the priests. This fellowship meal was a way of remembering the peace between God and his chosen people.

3. Sacrifices for the Forgiveness of Sins
Sin Offerings and Guilt Offerings

Sin made fellowship between God and his people impossible. These 2 types of offering were given by God to deal with this problem. It is not very clear which sins needed a sin offering to be made and which needed a guilt offering.

Read chapter 4:27-31.
How can someone be forgiven for their sin by an animal being killed?

What would happen if they sinned again?

If someone was not sorry for what they had done, do you think a sin offering would make them forgiven? (Psalm 51:16-17 might help.)

What is atonement?

Atonement is the action of bringing together two people or groups of people who are enemies and enabling them to be friends. In the Bible this usually means doing something about sin.

The Day of Atonement   Leviticus 16

It seemed that even the constant sacrifices of animals on the people's behalf could not stop the Tabernacle becoming tarnished with their sin. So once a year the High Priest had to carry out a special ceremony to make the Tabernacle clean again.

The High Priest needed a bull, a ram and 2 goats. First he had to wash himself all over and put on special linen garments. Then he had to take the bull and sacrifice it as a sin offering for himself and his family. He took a copper pot of burning coals from the altar, 2 handsful of incense and some of the bull's blood. Then he went behind the curtain into the Most Holy Place.

Once he was inside he sprinkled incense onto the coals to make some smoke so that he would not see the atonement cover of the Ark. Leviticus 16:13 suggests that, if he did see it, he would die. He took the bull's blood and sprinkled it with his finger on the atonement cover. Then he sprinkled some more, 7 times, in front of the atonement cover. The whole ritual was repeated, using one of the goats as a sin offering for the people.

In this way the High Priest was able to make the Most Holy Place a fit place for God to be, despite the sins of the priests and the sins of the people. The High Priest's job was very dangerous. By the time of Jesus he went into the Most Holy Place with a rope tied around his ankles, so that, if he was struck dead, he could be pulled out again!

When the High Priest came out from behind the curtain, he cleansed the bronze altar from the Israelites' sin by sprinkling the blood of the bull and the goat on it. It was then fit to be used for the sacrifices once again.

The Israelites' sin contaminated everything they came near, making it unfit for God. But God gave this way of making everything clean again, so that he could continue to live among his people.

The other goat had a different role; it was known as the scapegoat. The High Priest confessed all the wickedness and rebellion of the Israelites over the goat's head. Instead of sacrificing the goat, it was taken out into the desert and left there. The goat took the people's sins away from the camp, never to return.

The people's sin had to be taken away if they were to continue to live with God.

The man who took the scapegoat into the desert had to wash himself and all his clothes before he was allowed back into the camp. The High Priest had to wash himself too. Then he changed back into his ordinary priest's clothes and sacrificed the ram as a burnt offering for himself and the people. He burnt it on the altar along with the fat and the sin offerings.

The High Priest was someone who was able to do something on behalf of the people so that they could continue to live with God. In Hebrews 7:26-28 Jesus is described as a High Priest. Why does the writer to the Hebrews describe him like this? How was he different from the High Priest we have just described?

WEEK 10
Feasts

Preparation:
Read Leviticus 23:1-44, Matthew 26:17-30, using the Bible Study notes to help you.

Lesson Aim:
To learn the importance of regular times of remembering what God has done for his people.

Worship, for the Israelites, was a continuous way of life. Every day the commands of God had to be kept and every day, in the Tabernacle, sacrifices had to be performed so that God could continue to live with his people. It would be wrong for us to think that their worship of God was all sacrifice and rules; joyful praise and thanksgiving were very much a part of their lives. During the year there were special times when everyday life was interrupted and the whole nation gathered together to give thanks to God for his goodness to them.

These festivals were not thought up and organised by the people themselves; just like the instructions for the Tabernacle and the sacrifices, every detail of each festival was given to Moses by God. Only worship given in accordance with God's instructions was acceptable to God.

Leviticus

23:5   The Feast of Passover was linked with the Feast of Unleavened Bread and was the time when the people remembered their deliverance from Egypt. The last day of the feast of Unleavened Bread was called Firstfruits and celebrated the barley harvest.

23:15-22   The Feast of Weeks (or Pentecost) lasted for 1 day and came in the middle of the wheat harvest. It was a time when the people remembered the giving of the Law on Mount Sinai, it having taken approximately 50 days to reach there after leaving Egypt.

23:33-43   The Feast of Tabernacles lasted for 7 days and occurred at the end of the grape harvest. The Israelites made booths to live in and it was the time when they remembered the 40 years in the wilderness. This Feast, together with the Feasts of Passover and Weeks, were occasions when the people travelled up to Jerusalem for the celebrations. In New Testament times all adult Jewish males were expected to go to Jerusalem for these 3 feasts.

Matthew

26:17   The lambs were ritually slaughtered in the temple precincts and the meal took place in any house within the city bounds and in small companies. It was only following the destruction of the Temple in AD 70 that the ceremony reverted to a domestic one.

26:19   Preparation included checking that no leaven was present, providing a basin and towel for hand washing, and preparing the lamb, bitter herbs, unleavened bread and 4 cups of wine.

26:20   The Passover Meal. Before the meal ritual hand washing was strictly observed. The meal consisted of roast lamb, bitter herbs, unleavened bread, and 4 cups of wine at specified points. Prior to the 2nd cup of wine all the food was cleared from the table and the story of the Exodus was recounted as a dialogue between father and son (or suitable substitutes). The food was then brought back and part of the Hallel (Pss.113-118) was sung. This was followed by the 2nd cup of wine. Then came the breaking of the bread. (This was probably the point when Judas received his sop and disappeared, John 13:30.) This was followed by the 3rd cup of wine. The singing of the Hallel was then completed and the 4th cup of wine drunk (26:30).

Originally the meal was eaten standing, dressed ready for a journey (Exodus 12:11). That custom had been abandoned as a sign that the Jews were no longer slaves but free.

26:26   Jesus uses the bread to point forward to his coming death; in the Passover meal it was normally used to point backwards to the Exodus.

26:27   The 3rd cup of wine. For the new covenant see Jeremiah 31:31-34.

Bring in a photograph album containing pictures of specific events. Show the children the pictures and point out that, each time you see that picture, it reminds you of the event. If you did not have the photo you might forget about the event. In the same way God organised special times in the Jewish year to remind the people of the great things he had done for them in the past. Today we will find out about the special feasts that God instituted to make sure that his people did not forget what he had done for them. Teach the lesson, using the activity pages as a guide. Revise the memory verse.

If you do not have a photograph album, ask the children if they know their times tables and test them on the simple ones. Ask how they are able to remember them when they need them, bringing out the need for regular practice. What would happen if they did not practise them for 10 years?

Photocopy pages 56-59 for each child and add to the back of the activity book. If time permits celebrate a simplified Passover meal. The time required is 15-20 minutes.

Each small group requires:

- 1 candle plus matches

- 3 pieces of unleavened bread (Matzot, or pitta bread if Matzot unobtainable), placed one on top of another, separated by paper napkins

- Bitter herbs - use watercress or flat leafed parsley

- Small bunch of parsley and bowl of salt water

- Charoset - use applesauce mixed with cinnamon and raisins. It represents the mortar used in slavery in Egypt.

- Roast lamb (obtainable pre-packed from some supermarkets)

- 4 cups of wine - use red juice.

- Plastic plates, napkins, paper cup.

Sit in groups of 10-12 in a circle, with the candle in the centre. The leader's comments are in italic.

1. Recall the search for leaven and its removal.

2. Light the candle.

   Blessed are you, Lord God, who created light.

3. Fill the cup with red juice (first cup).

   God said: 'I will bring you out from under the burdens of the Egyptians.' Blessed are you, Lord God, King of the universe.

   Pass round the cup.

4. Dip parsley in the bowl of salt water.

   Remember the hyssop dipped in the blood of the lamb, which was painted on the lintel and doorposts.

5. Break the middle matzah in half and put half to one side on a napkin. Hold up the other half.

   This is the bread of affliction, which our fathers ate in the land of Egypt.

   Replace with other 2 matzot.

6. Fill the cup with red juice (second cup).

   God said: 'I will deliver you from out of their bondage.'

7. Youngest present asks -

   Why is this night different from all other nights?

   Reply -

   We were slaves to Pharaoh in Egypt, and the Lord our God brought us out with a mighty hand and an outstretched arm. If God had not brought us out we would still be Pharaoh's slaves.

8. Point to the various items on the table.

   What is the meaning of the lamb? It is the sacrifice of the Lord's Passover when he passed over our houses and slew the Egyptians.

   What is the meaning of the unleavened bread? Our fathers baked unleavened bread because they were thrust out of Egypt and could not wait.

What is the meaning of the bitter herbs? The Egyptians made our fathers' lives bitter with all kinds of hard work.

9. Raise the second cup of red juice.

   We thank you, O Lord, for delivering us from bondage.

   Pass round the cup.

10. Break the upper and middle half matzah into the required number of portions for each person in the group.

    Bless you, O Lord our God, King of the universe.

    Pass round.

11. Pick up bitter herbs and charoset.

    Blessed are you, O Lord our God, King of the universe.

    Dip watercress into the charoset, passing from person to person.

12. Break the lower matzah into the required number of portions and distribute with the remaining watercress. Pass round the lamb.

13. Break the remaining half matzah and distribute.

    Fill the cup with red juice (third cup).

    God said: 'I will redeem you with an outstretched arm'. Blessed are you, O Lord our God, King of the universe.

    Pass round the cup.

15. Fill the cup with red juice (fourth cup).

    God said: 'I will take you to me for a people'. Thank you, Lord God, that you are our King and our Saviour.

16. Pass round the cup.

    The remembrance of the Passover is now complete.

Feasts

Leviticus 23:1-44
Matthew 26:17-30

Worship, for the Israelites, was a continuous way of life. Every day God's commands had to be kept and every day, in the Tabernacle, sacrifices had to be performed so that God could continue to live with his people.

But it would be wrong for us to think that their worship of God was all 'sacrifice and rules'. Joyful praise and thanksgiving were very much a part of their lives. As well as people's own praise and thanks, there were special times when everyday life was interrupted and the whole nation joined together to give thanks to God for his goodness to them.

You might think that these festivals would have been thought up and organised by the people themselves, but they were not. Just like the instructions for the Tabernacle and the sacrifices, God gave every detail of each festival to Moses. Only worship ordained by God was acceptable to God.

There are 8 special feasts mentioned in Leviticus 23:1-44. Write them down in the order they are found in the passage.

1. ....
2. ....
3. ....
4. ....
5. ....
6. ....
7. ....
8. ....

The Sabbath (Leviticus 23:3)

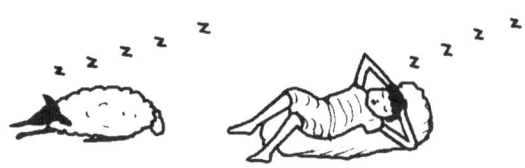

The Sabbath was an important part of life in Old Testament times. It was a time of rest and refreshment for everyone. Israelites, foreigners, slaves and even animals had a rest on the Sabbath (Exodus 23:12). Keeping the Sabbath as a separate day from all the others was one of the Ten Commandments God gave to Moses on Mount Sinai.

Which commandment is it? (The Ten Commandments can be found in Exodus 20.)

commandment number ....

Jesus upset the religious leaders because of the things he did on the Sabbath, which they said he should not do. Can you remember any of them? Instead of a simple day of rest, what had those religious leaders done to the Sabbath?

The Jewish Year

1 Nisan	2 Iyyar	3 Sivan	4 Tammuz	5 Ab	6 Elul	7 Tishri	8 March-esvan	9 Kislev	10 Tebet	11 Shebat	12 Adar

On the previous page you wrote down each feast next to a number. Read Leviticus 23:4-44 and, using those numbers, enter the feasts on the Jewish calendar.

The Passover

Passover was a time for the Israelites to look back and remember how God had rescued them from slavery in Egypt. God had sent plagues on the Egyptians so that Pharaoh, their king, would let the Israelites leave Egypt.

Can you remember what some of those plagues were?

The last of them was ...

The Plague on the Firstborn.

In every family in Egypt God made the eldest son die.

 the eldest son of the Israelite families did not die.

God had told the Israelites what to do.

Each family killed a lamb and put its blood on the door posts of their house. Then they ate the lamb. The Israelites' sons were spared because a lamb had died instead of them.

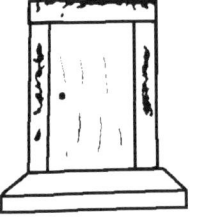

Pharoah was so shocked by this plague that he let the Israelites leave. The rescue had begun.

God gave Moses instructions for remembering the Passover before the plague on the firstborn took place! Exodus 12 tells us that it was to be celebrated as a festival to the Lord for all the generations who came after Moses.

In Matthew 26:17-30 we see Jesus and his disciples celebrating the Passover about 1300 years after Moses.

Where did Jesus and his disciples eat the Passover?

What was normally eaten at the Passover?

Jesus turned this Passover meal into a different kind of rememberance meal.

Read verse 26. Jesus broke the bread and said, 'This is ……… ………………'
Read verses 27-28. Jesus passed round the cup of wine and said, 'This is ……… ………………. which is poured out for many for the ………………………………… of ……………………….'

The lamb, which was eaten at Passover, was a kind of fellowship offering. It was killed in the Temple and its blood was poured out onto the sides of the altar. Jesus, by talking about his blood being poured out, was telling his disciples that he was going to be a sacrifice like the Passover lamb. Jesus' death was going to bring about a rescue even bigger than the rescue of the Israelites from Egypt. The Israelites were rescued from being the Egyptians' slaves and taken to the Promised Land, but Jesus was going to rescue people from their sinfulness and make them able to live with God, in heaven, forever.

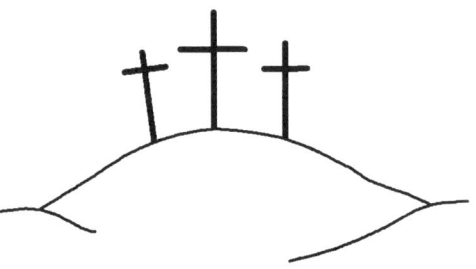

The church still celebrates this remembrance meal. What do we call it?

………………………………………………………………………

The Harvest Festivals

Three of the festivals celebrated events in the farming year.

The Feast of Unleavened Bread came directly after Passover. It, like the Passover, was a time to remember the rescue from Egypt. But the last day of the Feast of Unleavened Bread was a different festival, called **Firstfruits**, which marked the beginning of the barley harvest.

The Feast of Weeks (or Pentecost) celebrated the end of the barley harvest and the middle of the wheat harvest. It lasted one day and was a time when the people also remembered the giving of the Law on Mount Sinai.

The Feast of Tabernacles came at the end of the growing season. It was

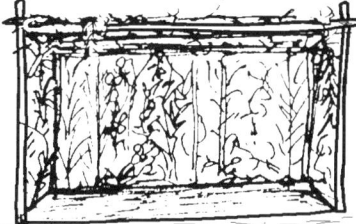

a celebration of the fruit harvest. The Israelites took branches and leaves and built themselves small huts out of them. These huts, or booths, were not at all strong or waterproof, but the Israelites had to live in them for 7 days so that they would remember how their forefathers had lived in the desert.

Other Feasts

The Feast of Trumpets was the first day of the especially solemn month of Tishri. Ten days later came the most solemn day of all ...

The Day of Atonement.

What can you remember about the Day of Atonement from the last lesson?

What did the High Priest have to do?

What did the Day of Atonement achieve?

The Israelites used these festivals to look back and remember what God had done for them, so that they would be joyful and thankful.

What has God done for you that you should thank him for?

WEEK 11
The New Covenant

Preparation:
Read Hebrews 8:1–10:14, using the Bible study notes to help you.

Lesson Aim:
To understand why the death of Jesus makes it possible for us to approach a holy God.

When God met with Moses on Mount Sinai he made a covenant with the Israelites. God promised that he would be their God and they would be his people. They had to keep his commandments, build the Tabernacle and perform sacrifices so that they could have their sins forgiven. However, there were 3 main problems. The Israelites could not go into God's presence - if they did they would die. The temple curtain made this very clear to the people. The second problem was the problem of sin. In spite of the daily sacrifices the people's sins remained. The third problem was the inability of the people to keep their side of the agreement.

8:1   By sitting down, Jesus demonstrated that his work of salvation was completed.

8:2   The true tabernacle set up by God is heaven.

8:4   Jesus would not be a priest on earth because he was from the tribe of Judah and the priests came from the tribe of Levi.

8:8-12   See Jeremiah 31:31-34.

9:4   In Exodus it is clear that the altar of incense was in the Holy Place, separated by the curtain from the Ark of the Covenant. It may be that the writer to the Hebrews stated it was in the Most Holy Place because of its function (Exodus 30:7-8, Psalm 141:2, Luke 1:10). In Revelation 8:3-4 the altar of incense in the new tabernacle is before the throne of God.

The jar of manna was kept in the Ark as a reminder of God's care and that God's people do not live on bread alone, but need God's word (Exodus 16:32-35, Deuteronomy 8:3). Aaron's rod was kept in the Ark as a sign that God had chosen him and so stop the grumbling of the rebellious (Numbers 17:10-11).

9:9-10   The old covenant with its sacrifices would only apply until the time of the new covenant. God's new covenant was not made because the old one had gone wrong. It was always God's intention to restore the relationship that Adam had broken by sending his son into this world to die on behalf of sinful people.

9:11   The greater and more perfect tabernacle is heaven (9:24).

10:5-7   See Psalm 40:6-8:

Cut out a simple figure from an OHP transparency and glue or mount on paper. Pin it up on a board and ask the children to say what sorts of things make this person unclean in God's sight. As they come up with suggestions mark the figure with splodges from a whiteboard marker. Remind the children that the sacrifices meant that God could continue to live among people who looked like that. However, since the destruction of the temple in AD 70, there have been no sacrifices. So how can God continue to live with his people? What is required to make them clean? Take a tissue, either cut in the shape of a cross or with 'Jesus' written on it using a permanent marker, and wipe the figure clean. Show them the tissue with the marks transferred to it. Only Jesus can make people really clean. In today's Bible passage we will find out why. Teach the passage, using the activity pages as a guide. Revise the memory verse.

Photocopy pages 61-63 for each child and add to the back of the activity book.

The New Covenant

Hebrews 8:1 – 10:14

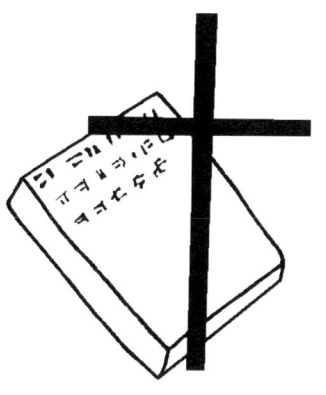

When God met with Moses on Mount Sinai, he made an agreement, or covenant, with the Israelites. God promised that he would be their God and they would be his people. They had to keep his commandments, build the Tabernacle, where he could live, and perform sacrifices to him so that they could be forgiven for their sins.

 — there were some problems with this covenant.

Problem No 1   No Entry   

Although the covenant was meant to make it possible for God to live among the Israelites, they could not meet God face to face or they would die. The temple curtain, which separated the Holy Place from the Most Holy Place, gave a clear message to the Israelites:

'You cannot come in!'

Read Hebrews 9:1-8. Why did God design the Tabernacle with a curtain like this?

Problem No 2   No Forgiveness

Despite the endless animal sacrifices, the Israelites' sin still remained with them. The sacrifices had to be done again and again and still the Israelites' sin made everything near them unfit for God. (Remember the Day of Atonement.)

Read Hebrews 9:9 and 10:1-4. What did the sacrifices achieve? (10:3)

Problem No 3   No Change

The Israelites were not able to keep their side of the agreement. They remained rebels, unable to keep God's commands.

Read Hebrews 8:8-9. What did God say he was going to do instead? (8:8) (*Write your answer on the scroll on the next page*).

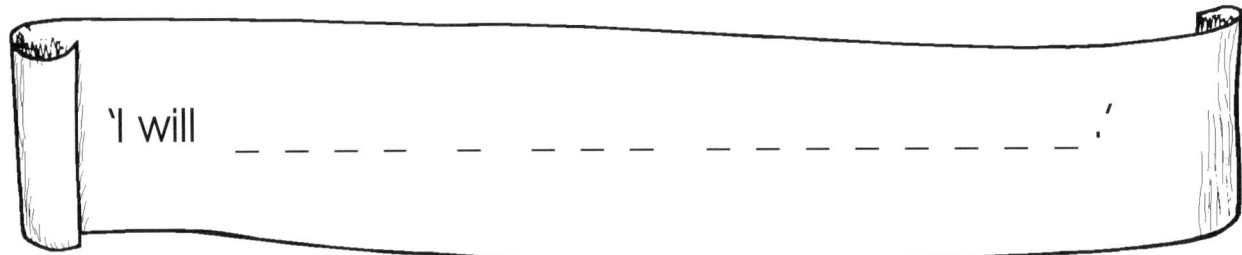

'I will _ _ _ _ _ _ _   _ _ _ _ _ _ _ _ _ _ _ _ _ .'

God did not make a new covenant because the old one had gone wrong. It was always God's intention to restore the relationship that Adam broke, by sending his son into this world to die on behalf of sinful people. As Hebrews 9: 10 says, the old covenant with its sacrifiices would only apply until it was time for the new covenant.

The New Covenant

Solved Problem No 1

Jesus' death **really has** made it possible for us to come into God's presence. When Jesus died something very strange happened. Read Matthew 27:50-51 and write down what happened.

....

The way to God had been opened up!

Solved Problem No 2

Jesus' death **really** took away sin. The High Priest had to keep on performing the same sacrifices in the Tabernacle, because they did not really take away sins. Read Hebrews 10:11-14. What was different about Jesus' sacrifice?

Solved Problem No 3

Along with real forgiveness and real fellowship with God, the new covenant brought a **real change** in people's hearts. In Hebrews 8:10-11 God promises to put his laws in the .... of his people and write them on their .... Although forgiven people are not perfect, (do you know any perfect Christians?), they WANT to obey God. One day they will be able to obey God perfectly - in heaven!

Quick Quiz!

Answer the questions and enter your answers in the grid.

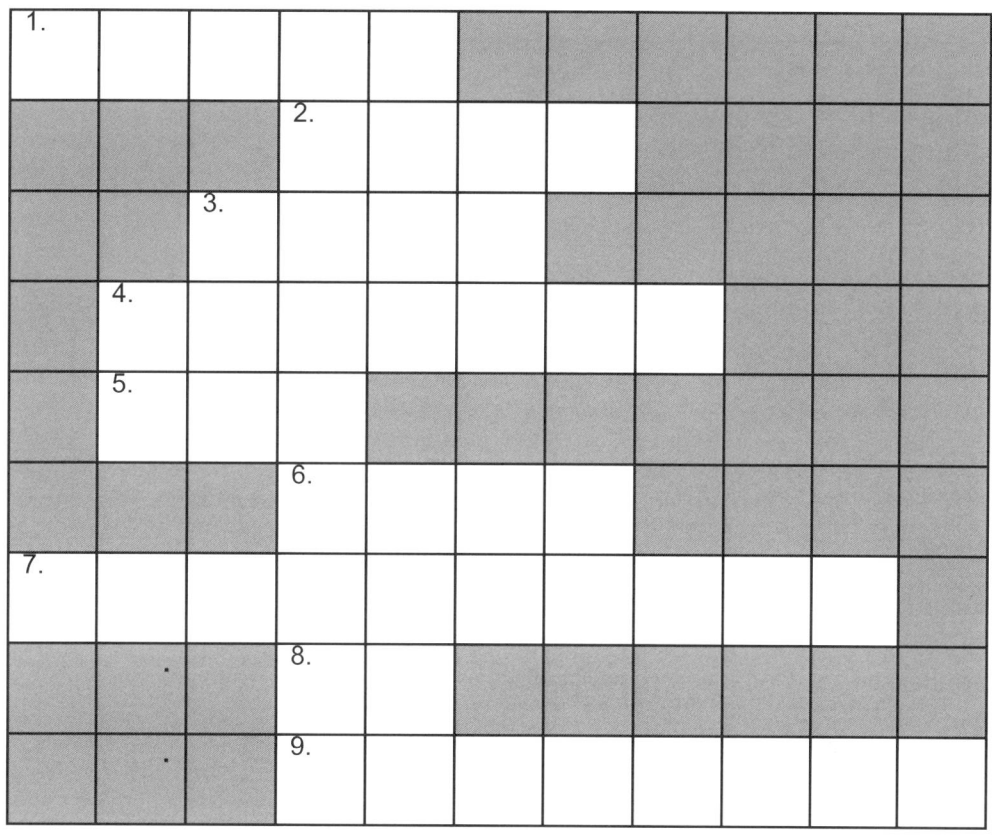

1. God gave Moses the Law on Mount _ _ _ _ _
2. The Tabernacle was a kind of _ _ _ _
3. The big problem with God living with his people is that God is h _ _ _,
4. ... and people are _ _ _ _ _ _ _
5. If a sinful person went into the Most Holy Place he would _ _ _
6. Jesus' death took away the sins of _ _ _ _ people (Hebrews 9:28).
7. Jesus' sacrifice was _ _ _ _ _ _ _ _ _ _ (Hebrews 10:10).
8. Could the blood of bulls and goats deal with sin?
9. The priests' sacrifices can never _ _ _ _ _ _ _ _ sins (Hebrews 10:11).

The letters in the fourth column spell _ _ _ _ _ _ _ _ _ _.

What does this word mean?

How is it possible for Jesus' death to do this?

What does each person need to do to be able to benefit from this new covenant?

WEEK 12
Daily Life

Preparation:
Read Hebrews 10:19-31, using the Bible Study notes to help you.

Lesson Aim:
To learn how we should worship God today.

The first 3 lessons in this series looked at what God told the Israelites about how they should worship him. When Jesus died and rose again this old covenant was no longer needed because the new one had replaced it. This lesson looks at the way the people of the new covenant were to respond to God and the difference this new way to God made to their daily life.

The passage has been printed on page 69 and is taken from the International Children's Bible, because this version is easier for the children to understand.

10:22   The first instruction is to draw near to God.

10:23   The second instruction is to hold firmly to our confidence in the new covenant. We can be certain of our forgiveness because we can trust God to keep his promises.

10:24   The third instruction is to encourage each other to love and good deeds.

10:25   The fourth instruction is not to give up meeting together.

10:26   This verse is addressed to people who have professed to be Christian and later decide to rebel against God and refuse to recognise him as God. Note the continuous present tense.

10:28   This is referring to Deuteronomy 17:6, which is part of a passage looking at the punishment for those of God's special people who refused to have God as their God.

10:30   See Deuteronomy 32:35-36.

Start by recapping on what worshipping God meant for the people of the Old Testament. What does worship mean for us today? Do we have to perform sacrifices? Why not? Do we have to keep festivals? Why / why not? Do we need a temple to worship in? Why not? Write down what they think comprises New Testament worship. Teach the Bible passage, using page 69 and the activity pages as a guide. At the end of the lesson go back over their ideas about New Testament worship to see how they compare to what has been discovered from the Bible passage. Revise the memory verse.

Photocopy pages 65-69 for each child and add pages 65-68 to the back of the activity book. Give out page 69 for use in class. The activity books can be taken home at the end of this session.

Prior to the lesson prepare a series of cards, each one containing some aspect of Christian worship that can be acted out. Divide the children into 2 or more small groups. The groups take it in turn to send one member to pick a card and mime it to their group. If the group guesses it correctly they get one point. If the group cannot guess the mime, the other group(s) are allowed to guess. Any group guessing correctly receives a point.

Daily Life in the New Covenant
Hebrews 10:19-31

We spent the first 3 lessons in this series looking at how God told the Israelites they should worship him. When Jesus died and rose again this old covenant was no longer needed because the new one had replaced it. But how should the people of the new covenant respond to God? What did this new way to God mean for the daily life of believers?
Read Hebrews 10:19-25.

The first instruction to the readers of this letter is in verse 22:

Come near to God.

This was something which was **possible / impossible** under the old covenant.

Remember the High Priest on the Day of Atonement. He was very scared as he entered the Most Holy Place. He took incense and the blood of the sin offering behind the curtain.

    What did he do with the incense?

    What did he do with the blood?

But we are .... to enter the Most Holy Place (10:19).

Jesus' body is like the curtain in that he is the way to God. When he died he made a way by which we could come near to God.

Verse 19 tells us that we can do this because of the blood of Jesus' death. We cannot come near to God without it - just as the High Priest could not enter the Most Holy Place without the blood of the sin offering.

We don't take Jesus' actual blood along when we pray to God. What do Christians mean when they talk about 'coming near to God through the blood of Jesus'?

So, unlike the early Israelites, we are able to come near to God without fear. Verse 22 tells us what we need to be like as we come near to God.

Can you find the 4 things mentioned?

1. a sincere ……………………………….

2. a sure ……………………………….

3. having been ……………………………….

4. washed with ……………………………….

Do you know what each one of these means?

The second instruction is in verse 23:

let us hold firmly

What are we to hold firmly to?

……………………………………………………………………………

We need to keep on believing that we are **really** forgiven through Jesus' death and that we **really** can be friends with the living God.

This letter was originally written to Jews, who were losing their confidence in the new covenant and were thinking of going back to the old ways. The writer of this letter wanted to assure his readers (and us) that they could be certain of forgiveness because they could trust God to do what he had promised.

Being a Christian is all about trusting God's promises. In the new covenant all we need to do is to accept God's wonderful gift of forgiveness and come near to him. It is easy to stop thinking of our forgiveness as a gift and start thinking of it as something we need to earn.

In the old covenant the person who brought a guilt offering actually saw the animal die instead of him. It would be easy for us to stop believing, because we can't see with our eyes that God has forgiven our sins. But as Hebrews 11:1 tells us, 'faith means knowing that something is real even if we do not see it.'

We must hold firmly to God's promise that Jesus' death has made us forgiven. We must not listen to anyone who tells us that we need something else as well.

The third instruction is in verse 24:

Let us .... **each other and** .... **each other** to show love and do good deeds.

The fourth instruction is in verse 25:

Do not stay away from ....

What does this passage say Christians should do when they meet together?

How might they do this?

What does this passage say to the person who says, 'I can be a Christian without going to church.'?

The Day in verse 25 means the Last Day, the day of judgment, when all people will have to stand before God and be judged. We know that this Last Day can come at any time following Jesus' return to heaven.

We don't know when it will be, but we know that every day it is getting closer and closer. Christians need to encourage one another to keep holding onto God's promises so we will be ready for that day.

Read verses 26-31. Here we have a severe warning.
This warning is to:

☐ those who have not yet heard the gospel.

☐ those who were once Christians but who now reject Jesus.

☐ those who are Christians, but still sin.

Under the old covenant, if it was proved by 2 or 3 witnesses that someone had refused to obey the law of Moses, they were put to death. Read Deuteronomy 17:2-7. Why was the punishment so harsh?

So what about those, who say they have been forgiven by God through the death of Jesus, but then go back to rebelling against him, who refuse to have God as their God or Jesus as their Saviour?

God is a just and holy God. Verse 30 tells us that he will judge his people. Since **all** of us do wrong things, we will **all** be judged, and the punishment for sin is death.

God has provided just **one way** by which we can be forgiven.

There is no other way; there never was. The old covenant, with all its sacrifices, was just a picture of the new covenant brought about by Jesus' once and for all sacrifice. The faithful people of God in the Old Testament were not forgiven by the blood of the animals they sacrificed, but they were benefitting in advance from Jesus' sacrifice, the one which really could take away their sins.

We have the opportunity to come near to the living God in a way that not even the High Priest could have dreamt of. Spend some time thanking God for this.

Let's also pray that we would be able to explain God's offer of forgiveness to our friends.

Hebrews 10:19-31

19 So, brothers, we are completely free to enter the Most Holy Place. We can do this without fear because of the blood of Jesus' death. 20 We can enter through a new way that Jesus opened for us. It is a living way. It leads through the curtain - Christ's body. 21 And we have a great priest over God's house. 22 So let us come near to God with a sincere heart and a sure faith. We have been cleansed and made free from feelings of guilt. And our bodies have been washed with pure water. 23 Let us hold firmly to the hope that we have confessed. We can trust God to do what he promised.

24 Let us think about each other and help each other to show love and do good deeds. 25 You should not stay away from church meetings, as some are doing. But you should meet together and encourage each other. Do this even more as you see the Day coming.

26 If we decide to go on sinning after we have learned the truth, there is no longer any sacrifice for sins. 27 There is nothing but fear in waiting for the judgement and the angry fire that will destroy all those who live against God. 28 Any person who refused to obey the law of Moses was found guilty from the proof given by two or three witnesses. He was put to death without mercy. 29 So what do you think should be done to a person who does not respect the Son of God? He looks at the blood of the agreement, the blood that made him holy, as no different from other men's blood. He insults the Spirit of God's grace. Surely he should have a much worse punishment. 30 We know that God said, "I will punish those who do wrong. I will repay them." And he also said, "The Lord will judge his people." 31 It is a terrible thing to fall into the hands of the living God.

Scripture quoted from the International Children's Bible, New Century Version (Anglicised Edition), copyright © 1991 by Nelson Word Ltd., Milton Keynes, England. Used by permission.

Job and the Problem of Suffering

Week 13   **JOB**   *Job 1:1 - 2:10; 38:1 - 42:17*
To understand that God is in control of every aspect of our lives and can be trusted.

Week 14   **THE PROBLEM OF SUFFERING**
To understand why suffering occurs and how the Christian should respond to it.

To understand that God is in control of every aspect of our lives and we can trust him to care for us in difficult situations.

The story of Job is about a good man who loses his possessions, health and children. His wife and friends interpret this as God's judgment on his sin and Job becomes an outcast. His friends explain his suffering in traditional religious terms (in Job's day material prosperity was a sign of God's blessing), but fail to offer Job any comfort or hope. Eventually God appears to Job - but not to answer his questions. Instead, God portrays his great power and might (38:1–41:34) and shows Job that his concept of God was too small. Job's reaction is to repent and worship (42:1-6). The book ends with God restoring Job's prosperity.

The story is about a real man (Ezekiel 14:14, James 5:11), who is thought to have been a contemporary of Isaac and Jacob - his wealth was tied up in livestock rather than money. He was a priest to his own family (1:5), which is another indicator that he lived before the time of Moses and the Levitical priesthood.

The book deals with the problem of suffering and God's sovereignty. If God is just and good, why does he allow the innocent to suffer? The only answer we are given is that God is all-powerful and there is nothing outside his control. Job did not understand why he suffered - but God enabled him to come through the time of trial.

This week's lesson concentrates on God's answer to Job, and is a preparation for next week's lesson, which deals with the problem of suffering, evil and pain. Any questions about the problem of suffering which are raised by the children should be left for the second week. It would be helpful if they are written down so that they do not get forgotten.

God said: 'My grace is sufficient for you, for my power is made perfect in weakness.'

2 Corinthians 12:9

WEEK 13
Job

Preparation:
Read Job 1:1 – 2:10; 38:1 – 42:17, using the Bible Study notes to help you.

Lesson Aim:
To understand that God is in control of every aspect of our lives and can be trusted.

1:1 Uz - exact location unknown.

1:4 These may have been birthday celebrations.

1:5 Job was aware that purity comes from the heart.

1:12 Satan's power is under God's control - he was only allowed to attack Job's possessions, not his person.

1:15 Sabeans - a group of nomadic raiders, who eventually settled in Sheba.

1:17 Chaldeans - nomads from South Mesopotamia (Abraham's homeland).

1:21 Job demonstrates his complete trust in God.

2:4-5 Satan says that Job is only really concerned for himself.

2:6 Again we see God in ultimate control of the situation.

2:11– 37:24
This needs to be summarised briefly for the children so that the story makes sense. e.g. Job's 3 friends told him that he must have done something wrong for God to send such suffering, but Job would not listen; he knew he had done nothing wrong.

31:35-37 Job wants to cross-question God ....

38:1-3 But God questions Job, causing a radical rethink by Job.

The only way Job can make sense of his suffering is to demonstrate that God is not wise and loving enough to always give us what we deserve, or, if he is wise, not just enough to do what is fair, or, if he is both wise and just, not powerful enough to control evil.

38:4 – 39:30
God details his loving care for the creation - both inanimate and animate. In this is shown God's wisdom in providing everything that is required for the world to function.

38:4-38 The marvels of the inanimate world:
- the earth (vv.4-7)
- the sea (vv.8-11)
- the dawn (vv.12-15)
- the underworld (vv.16-21)
- the weather (vv.22-30)
- the stars (vv.31-33)
- the clouds (vv.34-38)

38:39 – 39:30
The marvels of the animal kingdom.

40:1-14 God shows Job his moral power and demonstrates his concern for justice.

40:15 – 41:34
God demonstrates his absolute power - he can control what man cannot.

40:15 Behemoth - possibly the hippopotamus or elephant.

41:1 Leviathan - possibly the crocodile.

42:1-6 Job's reaction is to repent and worship.
NB. Job still does not understand why it all happened.

42:10-17 God vindicates Job by blessing him. (He was given twice as many animals, but the same number of children, as he had previously.) This does **not** teach that God's people will always be blessed on earth - our inheritance is in heaven (Hebrews 11:13-16, 2 Corinthians 5:1).

Lesson Plan

Talk about being stranded at a railway station or airport because your train or plane has been delayed. The only information you have is the screen or information board which shows the delay plus a short announcement over the public address system. It is only the people in the control room who have the big picture of what is happening. Link this with the idea of God having the big picture of our lives. He is the one who has complete control, which means that we can trust him through the bad and difficult times. In today's Bible passage we will find out what happened to a man who had many bad things happen to him and whether or not he continued to trust God.

Teach the Bible passage, using the activity pages to help you. Teach the memory verse.

Activities

Photocopy pages 73, 74 and 75 for each child. Use the pages to help the children understand God's answer to Job. This will be a useful basis for next week's discussion on the problem of suffering.

NB The activity pages are only an aid. If the class discussion follows a different line do not insist on their being completed. The important thing is for the children to understand that **God is in control of every aspect of their lives.**

Job - the Problem of Suffering

Job 1:1 – 2:10; 38:1 – 42:17

Job was a wealthy man with many possessions. In one day God allowed Job to lose - *(colour the appropriate boxes)*

friends	donkeys	house	servants
sheep	wife	children	
camels	health	oxen	lands

Did Job turn against God? (1:20-22) yes / no

What else happened to Job? (2:7) ....

Did that make Job turn against God? (2:9-10) yes / no

Did Job deserve the dreadful things that happened to him? (1:1; 2:3)

yes / no

Why did they happen?

73

Was it because God does not know everything that happens?

- ☐ God created the h _ _ _ _ _ _ and the e _ _ _ _, and put everything in it's right place (38:4-21).
- ☐ God controls the w _ _ _ _ _ _ _, and sends r _ _ _ on the d _ _ ground (38:22-38).
- ☐ God provides f _ _ _ for the animals and birds when they are h _ _ _ _ _ (38:39-41).
- ☐ God knows all about the a _ _ _ _ _ k _ _ _ _ _ _ (39:1-30).

So does God know and care about what is happening in his world?   yes / no

****

Was it because God is not just enough to do what is fair?

- ☐ God knows those who are p _ _ _ _ and w _ _ _ _ _, and they will be h _ _ _ _ _ _, c _ _ _ _ _ _ and b _ _ _ _ (40:8-14).

So is God just?   yes / no

****

Was it because God is not powerful enough to control evil?

- ☐ God controls the b _ _ _ _ _ _ _ _ (40:15-24).
- ☐ God controls the l _ _ _ _ _ _ _ _ _ (41:1-34).
- ☐ Man cannot c _ _ _ _ _ _ either.

So is God all-powerful?   yes / no

So . . .

why did God allow these things to happen to Job?
(1:6-12; 2:1-6)

74

Memory verse

Through his suffering, Job learnt something special about God.

Put the words of your memory verse into the grid below to make a crossword. Then write the shaded letters in numerical order into the spaces to discover from which book in the Bible the verse comes.

*Starting tip: place the longest word first and cross off the words as you use them. Remember to cross off **every** word made.*

He said to me, 'My grace is sufficient for you, for my power is made perfect in weakness.

2 _ _ _ _ _ _ _ _ _ _ 12:9

Did God tell Job the reason why all the bad things happened to him?

Did Job discover for himself why they had happened?

What can I learn from this?

WEEK 14
The Problem of Suffering

Preparation:
See lesson notes for relevant Bible passages.

Lesson Aim:
To understand why suffering occurs and how the Christian should respond to it.

As with all the apologetics lessons, the information in these notes is to be assimilated by the teacher, who can then decide on an appropriate presentation to the group. Last week's lesson on Job should have provided an introduction. The notes follow a suggested approach but you may want to vary it to suit your group.

INTRODUCTION

Divide the children into twos or threes and give each group a newspaper and a highlighter. Give them 5 minutes to look through the newspaper and identify every article about suffering. At the end of the exercise ask the children in what kind of ways people suffer in the world. Write their answers on a board or flip chart so that they can all see them. Aim to get the following answers:

disease, famine, natural disasters, war, job loss, bereavement, divorce, broken friendships, cruelty, guilt, poverty.

THE PROBLEM

If God is good and God is powerful why are innocent people allowed to suffer?

Is God not good enough?

Is God not powerful enough?

Some people use these arguments to say that God does not exist.

THE EXAMPLE OF JOB

Link with last week's lesson -

> how did Job suffer?
> did he know why he suffered?
> how did God answer him?

The secret things belong to the Lord our God, but the things revealed belong to us and to our children forever, that we may follow all the words of this law.
Deuteronomy 29:29

In Job we discovered that, because God is so much bigger than we are, there are some things that we will never understand about how he does things and why. But the things that have been revealed to us in the Bible are ours. The Bible tells us that God is loving and that he is faithful to all his promises. This means that we can trust him in the things that we do not understand. This week we are going to look into the Bible - God's revelation to us - and see what we have been told about suffering.

HOW SUFFERING CAME INTO THE WORLD
GENESIS 1-3

Ask the children the following questions, referring them to the appropriate Bible verses. Have the answers (A) already written out on strips of card so that they can be pinned up on the board.

1:31   What was all that God created like?
         A - all creation was good

1:26   What was special about man?
         A - man made in God's image

1:26   What responsibility was man given?
         A - authority to rule

1:28   What else do we learn?
         **A - man blessed
              made to be fruitful
              man to subdue the earth**

1:29   What else was given to man?
         A - plants for food

In the second account of creation we learn more about the blessings given to man.

3:8   The Garden of Eden was not just a nice place to live (2:8), it was special for another reason. God walked in his garden, so Adam

and Eve were living in the very presence of God.
A - able to be with God

2:15 What other blessing did God give Adam?
A - man given work

2:17 What else did God give Adam?
A - free will

This meant that God did not control him like a robot but allowed him to choose to obey God. This also meant he could choose to disobey God.

2:18 What else did God give Adam?
A - a helper

Man was put in a good situation.

What did man do with his free will? He rebelled against God. Instead of serving God he wanted to do things his own way and make himself the most important person in his life instead of God.

Because the man and woman rebelled against God, they brought God's curse on themselves. The blessings which he had given them were all changed. Go through the blessings pinned up on the board and write down beside them how they were changed.

all creation was good ➔ ground cursed (3:17)

man made in God's image ➔ death (3:19)

authority to rule ➔ never fully successful (3:17-18)

man blessed ➔ Adam and Eve cursed (3:16, 17)

made to be fruitful ➔ painful childbirth (3:16)

subdue the earth ➔ never fully successful (3:17-18)

plants for food can't ➔ subdue the earth (3:17-18)

able to be with God ➔ banished from God's presence (3:23)

man given work ➔ work became hard (3:17)

given a helper ➔ relationship problems (3:16)

When he was banished from God's presence man became utterly selfish. The one blessing not taken away from him was free will. Man was allowed to continue in his rebellion.

So, when Adam and Eve rebelled against God the good world that God had created changed forever. Paul, in his letter to the Roman Christians, described creation as 'groaning' and 'in bondage to decay' (Romans 8:18-22). Since the Fall there has been something terribly wrong with man and also with creation.

HOW DO THESE CURSES RELATE TO THE HUMAN SUFFERING THAT WE SEE TODAY?

On the board match up the following with the items written down in the introduction:

painful childbirth, relationship problems, ground cursed, work hard, work unsuccessful, can't subdue the earth, death, man utterly selfish, banished from God's presence.

WHY DOESN'T GOD DO ANYTHING ABOUT IT?

1. He has given man free will. Romans 1 says God has given man over to his sin - he lets man get on with it.

2. He can work his purposes through it. Suffering often makes people see their need of God. It also acts like a refining fire in the lives of those who do know God, making them more Christ-like (Romans 5:3-5, James 1:2-4, 1 Peter 1:6-7).

3. One day God will do something (Revelation 21:3-4) - he will come in judgment, and it will then be too late for men to repent.

SUFFERING AS A CHRISTIAN

As man rebels against God and hates him, man also hates those who follow God and bear his 'stamp' as Christians.

THE ETERNAL PERSPECTIVE

If this life were all there is it would be unfair. However, if God uses suffering to show people their need of him, they are in some senses more privileged than those who never see their need. We know that when Jesus comes again all wrongs will be righted (2 Thessalonians 1:5-10).

QUESTIONS

Try to refer back to the items on the board when answering questions.

FURTHER READING

The Problem of Pain   C.S. Lewis
A Grief Observed   C.S. Lewis

Bible Timeline

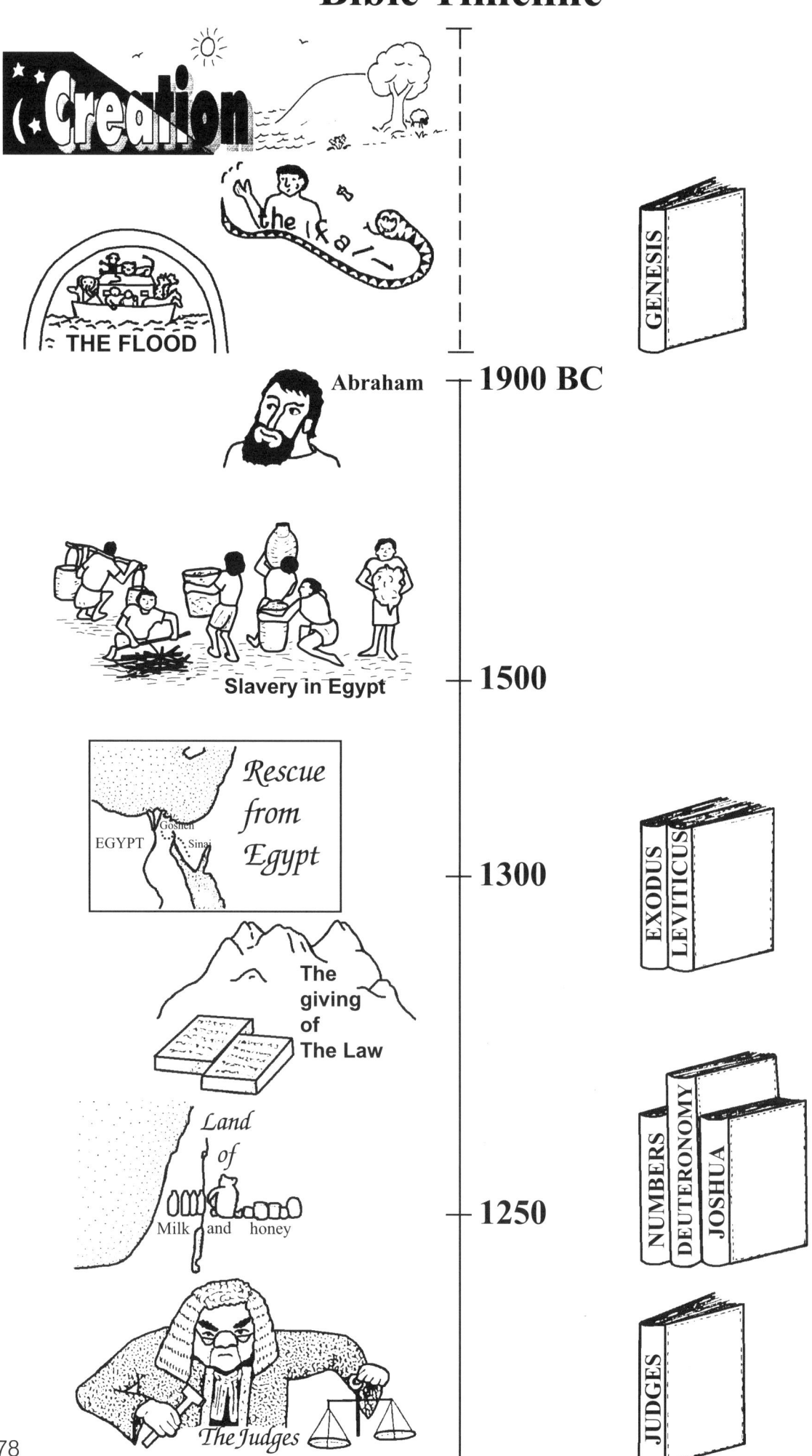

Syllabus for On The Way for 9-11s

	Year 1	Year 2
	Book 1 (18 weeks)	**Book 4 (18 weeks)**
Old Testament	Psalms (3) In the Beginning - God (5)	Psalms (3) Samuel (3) Proverbs (3) Return to the Promised Land (5)
New Testament	New Beginnings (6)	
Christmas	Prophecy Fulfilled? (4)	Christmas Questions (4)
	Book 2 (15 weeks)	**Book 5 (21 weeks)**
Old/New Testament	Life in Bible Times (5)	
New Testament & Easter	Investigating the Truth (10)	John the Baptist (2) Jesus is King (5) Peter (14)
	Book 3 (20 weeks)	**Book 6 (14 weeks)**
New Testament	The Early Church (4) Paul's Fellow-workers (3) Prayer (4) Parables (7) From Here to Eternity (2)	The Holy Spirit (6) The Existence of God (1)
Old/New Testament		How God Should Be Worshipped (5)
Old Testament		Job & The Problem of Suffering (2)

The books can be used in any order.
They contain differing numbers of lessons in order to fit the required number of weeks between Christmas and Easter and the following Christmas.
The number in brackets indicates the number of lessons in a series.

For more information about On The Way for 9-11s please contact:
Christian Focus Publications, Geanies House, Fearn, Tain, Ross-shire, IV20 1TW / Tel: +44 (0) 1862 871 011
or TnT Ministries, 29 Buxton Gardens, Acton, London, W3 9LE / Tel: +44 (0) 20 8992 0450

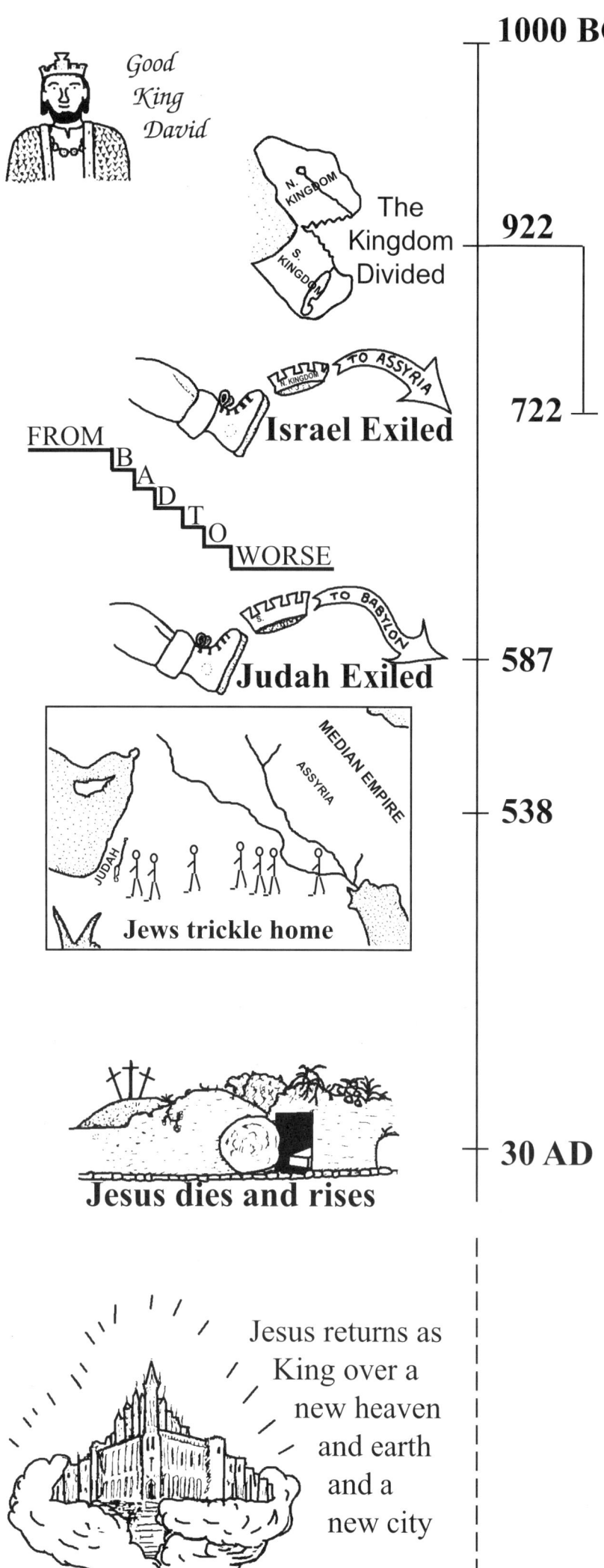